Cold Comfort Farm

A Play

Paul Doust

A SAMUEL FRENCH ACTING EDITION

FOUNDED 1830

SAMUELFRENCH-LONDON.CO.UK
SAMUELFRENCH.COM

ISBN 978-0-573-01737-7

www.samuelfrench-london.co.uk

www.samuelfrench.com

FOR AMATEUR PRODUCTION ENQUIRIES

UNITED KINGDOM AND WORLD EXCLUDING NORTH AMERICA

plays@SamuelFrench-London.co.uk

020 7255 4302/01

Each title is subject to availability from Samuel French,

depending upon country of performance.

COLD COMFORT FARM

First performed at The Watermill Theatre, Newbury, Berkshire on 11 June, 1991 with the following cast:

Flora Poste	Alison Larkin
Judith	Darlene Johnson
Elfine	Karen Westwood
Aunt Ada	Carol Gillies
Rennet/Mrs Hawk-Monitor	Diane Axford
Reuben	Steven Wickham
Amos/Sneller	Stephen Ley
Urk/Richard Hawk-Monitor	William Brand
Adam/ Mr Neck	Peter Cleall
Seth/ Charles	Ben Totterdell

Directed by Amanda Knott
Designed by James Merifield
Lighting by Lawrence T. Doyle

The role of Aunt Ada was subsequently played in this production by Dilys Hamlett

The action takes place at Cold Comfort Farm and the
gardens of Hautcouture Hall

ACT I

SCENE 1   The kitchen
SCENE 2   The kitchen
SCENE 3   The cowshed
SCENE 4   The kitchen
SCENE 5   The kitchen/Ada's room above
SCENE 6   The kitchen
SCENE 7   The meeting place of the Quivering
                  Brethren

ACT II

SCENE 1   The gardens at Hautcouture Hall
SCENE 2   The kitchen
SCENE 3   The cowshed
SCENE 4   The kitchen
SCENE 5   The kitchen
SCENE 6   Howling Church
SCENE 7   The kitchen

Time — 1930s

THE SET

The set consists of three principal areas: the kitchen, the upper level and the gardens at Hautcouture Hall. The kitchen and upper level are occasionally used for other purposes.

The kitchen

This area should be grotesque and disgusting, yet bizarrely real. The design of the kitchen can be addressed in various ways, but there are certain things which are essential to the action, including:

> A large wooden table and six chairs
> A fireplace and spit, with toasted water-voles on the spit
> A large sink
> Several doors (both interior and exterior)
> A large, old clock (and a new one later)
> A staircase leading to the upper level
> An enormous plant — the sukebind. This plant has broken through the floor in one corner of the kitchen. The top of it is swathed in chains and padlocks so that only the stalk is visible.

At the end of play the kitchen is completely transformed. It is wise to bear this in mind when designing the initial environment.

The upper level

This area is used chiefly as Ada's room and is somewhere above the kitchen. It should have something of the feeling of a "lair".

The gardens at Hautcouture Hall

These are exquisite, and everything that the kitchen is not. The two essential components of the gardens are a finely groomed lawn (on which the dancing takes place) and a grand and beautiful staircase leading down on to the lawn.

Anything else that provides a feeling of wealth, grace and opulence would be helpful.

CHARACTERS

The cast consists of two parts:

The Main Company

This is a central group of fifteen named characters. If numbers allow then all actors can play a single character; however, the number can be reduced to ten if necessary with the suggested doubling indicated below.

Flora Poste
Judith Starkadder
Elfine Starkadder
Aunt Ada Doom
Poor Daft Rennet/Mrs Hawk-Monitor
Reuben Starkadder
Amos Starkadder/Sneller
Urk Starkadder/Richard Hawk-Monitor
Adam Lambsbreath/Mr Neck
Seth Starkadder/Charles

The Chorus

This group of actors performs a variety of roles, including the Chorus, the Quivering Brethren, the County (at the ball and wedding; some of these have names which are given in the text) and additional Starkadders (for the Counting and wedding; some of these also have names which are given in the text). These groups can be expanded or contracted as necessary according to the availability of performers. The dialogue may have to be altered as a consequence of any such changes.

ACT I

SCENE 1

The kitchen at Cold Comfort Farm

When the CURTAIN *rises, a storm is brewing outside and there are long, slow, distant rumbles of thunder. A feeble wind whines about. Doors and windows rattle and bang. The lighting indicates the reddish and unnatural glow of a dying fire*

There is a sudden flash of lightning and a ferocious crack of thunder. Upstairs Ada screams, terrifyingly

Ada Argh! I saw something narsty! Narsty, narsty, narsty! I saw something narsty ... in the woodshed!

After more lightning and thunder there is relative quiet, followed by the sound of a bi-plane overhead. The plane lands, its headlamps illuminating the kitchen as it passes the window. Pause. There is a knock at the door. Pause. Another knock. Pause

Flora enters, wearing a large, fur-lined flying jacket. She carries a work-box, a suitcase, and a flying helmet. She looks about the room. Pause

Flora Oh, dear. (*To the audience*) And I cannot *endure* messes. (*She removes her jacket; underneath it she is fashionably and beautifully dressed*) Hallo? Hallo? Toasted water-voles? (*To the audience*) If only I'd remembered my copy of *Vogue*. A copy of *Vogue* is always so cheering — don't you think?

Charles enters. He too is in flying gear

(*To Charles*) Oh. What are you doing here?
Charles It's appalling, Flora. Quite appalling.

Flora Of course it's appalling. You must remember, Charles, we are in the kitchen of a Decaying Farm in a Theatrical Adaptation of a Classic Rural Novel. How could it be anything *but* appalling? What have you done with Mr Neck?

Charles He's waiting in the bi-plane.

Flora Then you must return to him at once.

Charles I can't. You know I can't.

Flora Charles — it's the plot.

Charles Need we really stick to it?

Flora Don't be absurd. One can't go experimenting willy-nilly with theatrical convention — it should lead to the most frightful mess. And what would the audience make of that?

Charles They might find it amusing.

Flora Nonsense. These adaptations are quite funny enough as it is.

Charles I wanted to say goodbye.

Flora We said goodbye. In the cockpit.

Charles Not properly. I couldn't. Not with Mr Neck sitting between us. I should have had the uneasy feeling that he were noting down our dialogue.

Flora Of what possible interest could be our conversation to Mr Neck?

Charles Well, he did mention, didn't he, that his next production is to be ... a romance?

Lightning. Thunder

This must be just about the foulest winter of the nineteen-thirties.

Flora Probably.

Charles I shall send you some gum-boots.

Flora Gum-boots?

Charles If things turn really nasty. You'll get terribly muddy stomping about those fields.

Flora Charles, my dove, you really mustn't fuss about me so. Things will certainly turn extremely nasty. They always do. But it would take "nasties" of the most unspeakable kind before I should even think of turning to gum-boots for protection. They're so frightfully unfashionable. Besides — I don't stomp.

Charles Don't you?

Flora No. I step.

Charles Is there a difference?

Flora Oh, really Charles — there's a *world* of difference!

Charles Don't ask me to leave you here, Flora. Don't. It's an impossibly wretched request!

Flora If you don't take off again soon this storm will make it quite impossible.

Charles I'll manage.

Flora I hope so.

Charles You're blushing.

Flora It's the cold.

Charles You have the most beautiful golden hair.

Lightning. Thunder

Come back with me to London. Please!

Flora Charles — I *can't*! I have, as you know, been recently orphaned of both parents — I am, after all, the Heroine of this piece — and though my father, Robert Poste, was always spoken of as a wealthy man, he has been found, on his death, to be a poor one. This means that my only inheritances are, from my father, a strong will, and from my mother, a slender ankle. As for money I have but one hundred pounds a year. And I cannot play bridge.

Charles That doesn't mean you have to come and live here.

Flora Who else am I to turn to? Oh no, Charles. Distant Relations are one thing — but I should never impose upon a friend.

Charles I had hoped, Flora, that I was a little bit more than a friend.

Flora And anyway — I want my rights! (*She takes a letter from her workbox and hands it to Charles*)

Ada screeches upstairs

Oh, really — who is that screeching? I do not approve of people who screech.

Charles (*reading*) Cold Comfort Farm, Howling, Sussex.

Lightning. Thunder. The voice of Judith

Judith (*off*) Dear Cousin, so — you are after your rights at last! Well, we have expected to hear from Robert Poste's Child these last twenty years.

Charles Robert Poste's Child?

Flora That's me. Quaint, isn't it?

Judith (*off*) My man once did your father a great wrong — but you must never ask me what it was ...

Flora My lips are sealed.

Judith (*off*) My lips are sealed! Child, child! If you come to this doomed house, what is to save you? Your affectionate cousin,

Flora Judith Starkadder.

Charles Judith Starkadder?

Judith (*off*) Judith Starkadder ...

Lightning. Thunder. Flora takes the letter and replaces it in her work-box

Charles Who are these Starkadders, exactly?

Flora The offspring, apparently, of my mother's antique sister — Ada Doom. The antique herself will quite certainly be dead by now — which is just as well. When only a child, you see, Aunt Ada had a very unfortunate experience — in a woodshed. Henceforth, she became a total recluse. I should not have approved of Aunt Ada.

Charles Who do you approve of?

Flora Almost no-one. And those who insist on approving of me, Charles, only do so because they think I look serious.

Charles I don't believe you're serious in the least.

Flora Then you are quite mistaken. I am entirely serious about almost everything. Especially Miss Austen.

Charles Miss Austen? The novelist?

Flora Miss Austen, you see, liked everything to be tidy and pleasant and comfortable about her; and so do I. For unless everything is tidy and pleasant and comfortable about one, a person cannot even begin to enjoy life.

Charles And that's your plan, is it? To tidy up this farm and to make the life of its inhabitants quite pleasant and comfortable?

Flora Indeed. And what more exciting a prospect could a Heroine possibly have? There will, of couse, be moments of hiatus — but The Descriptive Narrative will serve as a diversion.

Charles Descriptive Narrative?

Flora Intoned, as it always is, by some lumpen group of otherwise redundant performers, dramatically addicted to the art of choral speaking. It's quite hilarious!

Charles And will there be a distracted, female sleepwalker?

Flora Inevitably.

Charles Her name?

Flora Rennet.

Charles Mad?

Flora Barking.

Charles Striding through the small hours in badly fitting nightwear?

Flora What else? Lunatic somnambulance goes hand-in-glove with the rag-bag chemise. Besides, Nature, quite certainly, will have curdled in her veins — and once curdled in the veins of any young woman Nature lays waste all sense of personal grooming. Then, of course, there will be Seth!

Charles Seth?

Flora Son of Judith! Ferociously highly sexed and quite deliciously absurd! Or possibly Reuben.

Charles Reuben?

Flora Sometimes even Urk.

Charles Urk!?

Flora But oh, I do hope not; not an Urk. A Seth, you see, will at least be ornamental, a Reuben charming, but Urks are both ugly and entirely impolite.

Charles Well ... should it ever get too much for you — you will telephone me, won't you?

Flora Thank you, Charles — but it will never get too much for me. I have in my work-box, you see, two of the most useful books in the world. One, *The Higher Common Sense* — surely the wisest anthology of Civilized Thought ever compiled? — the other, Miss Austen's novel, *Mansfield Park*. The first will provide me with guidance in my labours, the second with refreshment when my work is done.

Charles You really are the most wonderful creature.

Flora I think you should go now, Charles — before Mr Neck bursts in, at a wholly inappropriate moment, speaking an enthusiastic and strangely uninterrupted monologue, bristling with plot, which the audience, poor things, will be obliged not only to listen to, but to digest.

Charles Flora — you do know how I feel about you, don't you? Don't you?

Neck enters

Neck Hey, Charlie baby ...!

Flora (*to the audience*) Mr Neck.

Neck I've been out in that bi-plane nearly ... Oh, now wait a minute! Wait a minute! Gee, but this'd make some location! Boy, *what* a location! I've got to come back here sometime — when I've found myself my new actor! Flora sweetheart — speak to your folks here for me will you? Tell 'em a big Hollywood producer wants to shoot a picture. Tell 'em I'll pay anything! Anything! Hey, that's it! I'll send 'em on a vacation of a lifetime! The South of France! The hotel *I'm* staying at, OK? (*He produces a brochure and hands it to Flora*) The Hotel Miramar! See? Just look at the life they lead out there! All those old dames just lying around in the sun? You put an old bird on the side of that pool — and she feels a million years younger. Oh, yes! I seen it happen! I tell you babes, there's only one place in this whole world near half as beautiful as the Hotel Mirimar — and that's right here in Sussex. Hautcouture Hall! I met the family on this Search of a Star, stuff. I was looking for someone English, you know, but earthy. So I fixed to test the kid — Dick. Richard Hawk-Monitor. But it didn't work out. Not that he wasn't a dish! Oh, boy — what a dish! But he was too damned ... *British*. See? British Reserve. And British Reserve is *not* what they want. Not anymore. No — what they want now is *Passion*! I want a fella who can take that screen in the palm of his hand and have the dames just melt right through the floor! A big, husky stiff! Red blood! I need a guy who looks great in a tuxedo — but even better half out of it! Know what I mean? Hence — I gotta go to France! Well I've looked every other place! And if I don't find him soon, I'm sunk! So — come on now, Charlie! Wake up! Smell the coffee! I've *hired* you and your wings to fly me over there, haven't I? Let's fly! Know what I mean? So long, toots — see you again!

Neck exits

Charles produces a magazine

Flora A copy of *Vogue*?
Charles I thought you might find it ... cheering.

She takes the magazine

There's a fascinating piece on Fanny Ward.
Flora Fanny Ward?
Charles The child star of the musical comedy theatre.
Flora But I thought her a total recluse?
Charles She has re-emerged, apparently, at the age of ninety-six, as gay as champagne and lovelier than ever.

Flora "Beauty and Joy for Those No Longer Young" ... Oh, how splendid!
I shall have no time to read this, of course; I shall be far too busy. But
I shall place it, for safe keeping, in the bottom of my work-box.
Charles Along with the copy of *Mansfield Park, The Higher Common
Sense* and Mr Neck's brochure for the Hotel Miramar?
Flora Run along now, Charles. Please.

Charles makes to go

Oh, and Charles?
Charles Yes?
Flora Don't forget to feed the parrot.
Charles What parrot?

She laughs a little and turns away

Charles exits

Flora Oh, any parrot — bless you, my love.

We hear the plane take off and disappear. Flora glances at the copy of
Vogue, *then places it with the hotel brochure in her work-box. As she does
this she sees the letter. She takes the letter and looks at it*

(*To the audience*) Judith Starkadder! The name itself is most promising
of amusement! She's simply bound to have a shock of tangled black
hair, resembling, of course, a nest of snakes, a voluminous scarlet shawl,
stained, no doubt, in the blood of her grief, and will almost certainly be
given to mooning about at night with a flickering candle and only her
loneliness for company. Her husband, I am sure, will be called Amos;
and if he is you know what he will be like. But — back to the plot! The
timeless leaden day merges imperceptibly towards eve.

The Lights change abruptly to a bleakly-waning-moon effect

(*To the Lighting Box*) Thank you.

SCENE 2

The same. The kitchen clock begins to chime

Flora (*to the audience*) Well, at least the clock's working.

The clock explodes

Oh.

Judith (*off*) Who's that? Who's there?

Flora (*to the audience*) I could, of course, ask the same question ——

Judith (*off*) Who is it that breaks into my sorrow?

Flora (*to the audience*) — if I didn't already know the answer.

Judith (*off*) And I with only my loneliness for company ... Son?

Flora (*to the audience*) Oh dear ...

Judith (*off*) Is it you?

Flora (*to the audience*) I fear *I* shall be quite a let-down.

Judith (*off*) Is it you — child of my wretched body ?!

*Judith enters with a "flickering" battery-operated candle. She has
tangled black hair and a scarlet shawl*

Flora How do you do? I'm Flora Poste. You must be my cousin Judith.
(*She puts out her hand*)

Judith stares

Is my lipstick the wrong shade?

Judith stares

I wonder — would you think me terribly rude if I went straight up to my
room? I really am very exhausted.

Judith My son — Seth; his brother — Reuben; and my nephew — Urk;
They are all waitin' to meet their cousin. Well ... Urk and Reuben,
anyway.

Flora Why? Where's Seth?

Judith moans and shrinks back

Oh. Well in that case I shall *certainly* go to my room. (*To the audience*)
Judith's magnificent shoulders rise and fall in a slow, billowy shrug
which agitates her breasts.

Judith As you will. (*She makes to exit*)
Flora One moment. You don't have a telephone, do you?

Judith stares

No, I thought not. Then would you be a lamb and just pop out to the post box for me? (*She produces a postcard and pencil. She writes*) "Dear Charles ... Worst fears realized. Seth, Reuben *and* Urk. Send gumboots." There. Now, my room is this way I take it?

Flora takes the candle and exits

A door is blown open by a gust of wind. There is a lurid red glow from the fire. Lightning. Thunder

Seth enters. He wears mud-spattered boots and a sweat-laden, torso-clinging shirt. He laughs

Seth Well, mother mine — 'ere I am. I told 'ee I'u'd be back for my porridge — an' I 'ave kept my word ...
Judith These middocks 'ave been in the snood since afore breakfast time! Where 'ave you been?

Seth laughs and peels off his shirt

Rennet enters, sleepwalking

Seth? Seth!
Seth I 'ave been to the picture 'ouse — wi' Mark Dolour.

Rennet stops

Judith Mark Dolour?

Rennet starts, distractedly

Seth Aye — Mark Dolour!

Rennet exits

Judith Cur! Coward! Liar! Libertine!

Seth lounges towards the fire. Judith recoils with a moan. Seth wrenches a water-vole from the spit

> Picture 'ouse? Ha! Who 'ave you been a-mollocking this night? Moll at the mill or Violet at the vicarage? Or Ivy, p'haps, at the iron mongery?

Off stage, Rennet gives a piercing screech, which is followed by a great splash of water

> Seth — my son ... my son ... Do you want to break your mother's 'eart?

Seth Yes. (*He sinks his teeth into the vole*)

Lightning. Thunder. Black-out. We hear Ada screaming during the black-out

The Chorus enters and the storm subsides

SCENE 3

The cowshed. The Chorus is on stage. Adam is also on stage, carrying a bucket and a wooden leg. The Lights come up gradually during the following to a sallow-dawn effect. NB This choral passage (and indeed all choral passages) is entirely up for grabs. It can be delivered in whatever way thought most effective, as long as it is kept within the manner of the production

Chorus Dawn creeps over the downs like a sinister white animal. Cold Comfort Farm, like a beast about to spring, is crouched on the bleak hillside, whence its fields, fanged with flints, drop steeply to the village below. A growing viscous light invades the sky.

Adam comes forward with the bucket and wooden leg. A great deal of "milking" goes on here

Adam (*singing*) Rooksies and Barnsies
        Do fly 'ome like charmsies,
        And the Tigget nor Teazle
        Mun chaff nor the winde.

Chorus From the reeking interior of the cowshed comes the mindless crooning of an ancient voice. It is half-past six on this winter morning and ——

Adam (*to the audience*) Adam Lambsbreath,

Chorus — the hired hand, is about the task which he has performed at this hour and in this place for the last eighty years or more. The gnarled fingers of ——

Adam (*to the audience*) Adam Lambsbreath,

Chorus — mechanically stroke the teat of Graceless. Graceless! the big Jersey with the wooden leg. Graceless! whose wooden leg is working loose ... The other cows, Feckless, Aimless and Pointless, stand with their heads lowered dejectedly against the hoot-piece. There is a close bond, a slow, deep, primitive, silent, down-dragging link between ——

Adam (*to the audience*) Adam Lambsbreath

Chorus — and all living beasts.

Adam (*to the audience*) We know each other's simple needs.

Chorus He leaves the cowshed ——

Adam moves away

— and Graceless ——

The wooden leg falls

— falls over.

The Chorus exits

SCENE 4

The kitchen. The Lights come up to a stifled-morning effect

Adam Aye, the dumb beasts niver fail a man. They niver fail a man as does — a child ...

Elfine enters with a bunch of twigs

Elfine!

Elfine shrinks back, and then presents the twigs to Adam

My cowdlin'!

Elfine darts away

   Urk enters carrying dead mammals

Urk Ha!
Elfine Oh!
Adam Urk!
Reuben (*off*) Adam!

   *Elfine exits, wailing. Reuben enters carrying the scranlet and the
   wooden leg*

We hear pained lowing from Graceless, offstage

   Graceless 'as lost 'er leg!

Urk laughs and impales a mammal on the spit

   Who will pay money for 'er now? Who wants a cow wi' only three legs?
Adam Nay, niver talk o' sellin' our Graceless, Mus' Reuben! 'Twould
   break my heart to loose her!
Reuben Aye, mun be it would; but I'd sell 'er all the same ——

Adam wails

   — if so be as someone 'ud take 'er. But they woan't, will they? Aye, 'tes
   all one. Cold Comfort stock ne'r finds a buyer. Wi' the Queen's Bane
   blighting our corn, and the King's Evil laying waste the clover ...
Urk ... and the Prince's Forfeit a-sucking at the teats o' the sows!
Reuben Aye, 'tes the curse! But the least I can do is to fix our Graceless's
   leg!
Adam Leave 'er be! A beast needs solitude, same as a man does! I'd take
   shame to myself, Mus' Reuben, to watch over them animals like you do
   — a-countin' every blade of sporran and middock of chaff as the poor
   critures eat!
Reuben And what if I didn't? Who else cares a jot about this farm?

Adam Your father, that's who! 'E be still alive, Mus' Reuben and —
Reuben I warn 'ee, Adam — when father dies and I *am* in charge o' this
farm ——
Urk Ha!
Reuben Urk!

*Flora enters, wearing another fashionable outfit. She carries a pair of
net curtains and her work-box*

Flora I say — would you mind not talking quite so loudly, please? I have
only just woken up. (*To the audience*) Silence, emphatic as a thunder-
clap, follows my request.

Adam passes Flora with a tray

(*To the audience*) Four sausages, a crocket of marmalade, porridge, five
fried tomatoes, a kipper, a fat pot of black tea — and nine boiled eggs?

Judith enters

Judith You mun take 'er food up now.
Flora Whose food?
Urk Ha!
Judith And don't forget 'er bread. (*She takes the loaf from the table, cuts
a thin slice, and puts it on the table. She puts the rest of the loaf on the
tray*)

Adam exits

Flora stands up an overturned chair

Reuben Nay, niver sit there, Robert Poste's Child!
Flora Why on earth —— ?

*There is a blast of wind through the door as Amos enters with a
warming-pan*

(*To the audience*) A huge body; rude as a wind-tortured thorn.
Judith Husband?

Flora (*to the audience*) Amos.
Amos Rennet!
Flora Where?

Rennet enters —wet

Ah ...
Amos Take my warmin'-pan!
Flora Warming-pan? (*To the audience*) Could he be a member of some bizarre religious sect?
Amos And bring the bowls!

Rennet takes the pan and keeps it with her for the rest of the scene. Amos sits. Rennet brings some bowls, spoons, etc. to the table and serves them porridge, messily

Flora (*to the audience*) Rennet, more daft than even I had expected, goes about her task in what is known as The Tortured Dumb Beast manner. Judith, of course, is at the door — gazing blankly through the fetid air which hangs over the farm like a sallow lemon. Twin rods — Anguish and Grief — jut from her eyes like frozen fountains. And on these chilly peninsulas flap the tattered rags of a mangled passion. (*To Judith*) Cousin Judith — about my one hundred pounds ...
Judith Keep it! Keep it! We'll niver touch one half-penny o' Robert Poste's money! You are our guest. Every middock you eat is paid for by our sweat!
Flora Oh, all right then.

Judith sits at the table. The thin slice of bread is passed about

Seth enters

Judith moans

Amos Woman!

Seth moves to the table and takes a bowl, but does not sit. He lounges with the bowl a little way off. Rennet messily delivers some porridge to Seth and then retreats to the sink

Flora (*to the audience*) Seth does not touch his porridge. Judith makes only a pretence at eating hers — idly patting it up and down and forlornly building castles with the burnt bits. Her eyes rest on her son as he sprawls in the lusty pride of his casual manhood. Secrecy pouts her full mouth. Seth takes a pack of cards from his trouser pocket and glances at them, stealthily. The cards have pictures — and the pictures are of women. (*She apprehends Rennet*) Excuse me, my dear, but has Nature, by any chance, curdled in your veins?

Rennet nods

Yes, I thought so. And why? Were you disappointed of a man?

Rennet nods

Mmm ... That's what usually does it. What was his name?

Rennet looks distracted

Oh. Have you lost the power of articulate speech, then? Is that all part of having gone daft?
Amos Aye! As is 'er godless habit o' throwing herself down the well!
Flora Down the well?
Seth Aye. Wheniver she 'ears 'is name ——
Judith No!
Seth Mark Dolour!

Rennet starts wildly and exits

Seth laughs

Amos Devil creature!
Reuben Father ...
Amos 'Old your peace!
Flora (*to the audience*) And Reuben, though a fierce tremor rushes through his mighty form, holds it.

Pause. We hear Rennet screech off stage, followed by a splash

Amos My warmin'-pan!

Amos exits

Seth laughs and looks across the kitchen out of a door. He loosens some clothing

Judith Seth, my son ...!
Seth 'Ere — you!

Off stage there is a delighted whoop from a woman

Judith My son!
Flora (*to the audience*) But Seth, indifferent to his mother's pitiful plea, strides out purposefully into the fecund air.

Seth exits

(*To the audience*) He fails to notice, however, that he's dropped one of his picture cards.

She picks it up

Off stage there is a squeal of joy from the woman, and gasping from Seth

Who on earth is that?
Reuben It dunnay matter who she is — Seth'll mollock 'em all!
Flora Mollock?
Urk Ha!
Flora But what on earth does it mean to "mollock"?

More noises off stage. Judith moans and collapses, her face in the porridge

Oh, I see ...

There is pained lowing from Graceless, off stage

Urk and Reuben stand

Just a moment — you haven't finished your breakfast, yet.

Urk Ha!

Reuben Brikfist?! Brikfist?! There's swedes t'be chopped an' legs t' be mended! A farm doan't swaddle itsel'!

Flora I'm sure it doesn't, but ... (*indicating the scranlet*) I say, what's that? Some sort of antique?

Reuben Anteekie?! Anteekie?! Nay — 'tes a scranlet!

Flora A scranlet?

Reuben I did scranlet three 'undred furrows, down i' the bute! Aye—and afore daybreak, too! *Three 'undred!* Could you ha' done that?

Urk Ha! He do think you be after farm!

Flora What? Oh, really, Reuben. I wouldn't care if the bute wasn't scranleted at all — really I wouldn't. I'd let ... I'd let you do it all instead.

Urk Ha!

Reuben Lit?! Lit?! A mirksy, flibberdy word as to use to a man as 'as nursed this farm like a sick mommet — a man as knows ivery inch of soil and patch o' sukebind i' the place ...

Flora Sukebind?

Reuben Lit?!

Urk Ha!

Flora Oh, do stop that dreadful ha-ha-ing, Urk!

Pause

Urk exits

Cousin Reuben — we really must get this straight. I don't want the farm. Really I don't. I know nothing at all about agriculture. Why, just think of the mess I should make of the sukebind — whatever the sukebind is. No, I would much rather leave all that to people who do know something about it, like you. Really I would.

Reuben stares at Flora

He exits, leaving the door open. Adam enters with the empty tray

Again there is pained lowing from Graceless, off stage. Flora closes the door

Adam Nay! Niver do that, Robert Poste's Child.

Flora Who *did* you take that food to?

Adam (*opening the door*) I be watchin' for my mommet — my liddle Elfine.

Flora And what is the sukebind?

Adam Sometimes ... sometimes she goes up to Howchicker Hall.

Flora Who does?

Adam Elfine!

Flora Oh. Oh, Hautcouture! The Hawk-Monitors' place.

Adam moves to the sink and begins to clean the dishes with the bunch of twigs

Adam Days she'll be away, sometimes; a-wanderin' on the 'ills!

Flora But why does she go up there?

Adam No company but the teazle. No creature to protect 'er but the marsh-tigget. My liddle Elfine, who I did cowdle in my own arms! Did cowdle in my arms when ——

Flora When she was but three days old and as blind as a raspberry; quite. But about Hautcouture Hall ... I say, you could do that much more easily with a little mop, you know. A little mop with a handle?

Adam I don't want no liddle mop wi' no 'andle! I been cletterin' wi' thorn twigs these last siventy years! I don't want no liddle mop!

Flora Then I shall send for one immediately. (*She lifts Judith's head and removes the porridge bowl*) I don't suppose you have a cinnamon wafer, do you? I'm not too fond of porridge, you see. Oh, and something I might use as a table cloth? A piece of clean newspaper would do.

Adam We've troubles enough at Cold Comfort Farm, Robert Poste's Child, wi'out bringin' in no gurt old newspaper to upset and fritten us!

Flora Troubles? (*She replaces the bowl*) What sort of troubles?

She releases Judith's head, which thuds into the porridge bowl

Adam I tell 'ee, Robert Poste's Child — there's a curse on Cold Comfort Farm!

Flora A curse? Oh, you mean that the seeds do wither as they fall into the ground, and the earth will not nourish them? Then why don't you leave?

Adam Leave? Nay — 'tes impossible for any on us t'leave! Mrs Starkadder, she be sot on us stayin'. 'Tes 'er life; 'tes the blood in 'er veins!

Flora Cousin Judith? But she doesn't seem too happy here herself.
Adam   Nay, Robert Poste's Child. I mean the *old* lady — *old* Mrs
  Starkadder ... (*He indicates the ceiling*)
Flora Aunt Ada Doom? But she's dead.
Adam   Diid?! Diid?!
Flora As a door-nail, surely?
Adam   Ha! Ada Doom's not derd! She'm aloive!
Flora Alive?
Adam   Aye — aleeve! And her 'and do lie on us like an 'ammer on toad-
  stool. But she'm niver left this farm these sivinty years! She'm niver
  leaves her room, even — but once a twelve month, that is. And then only
  for The Counting ...
Flora The Counting?

*There is a thud from upstairs and a wail from Ada. Adam takes the wooden
leg*

Adam   I mun fix our Graceless's leg.
Flora But ...
Adam   Leave me in peace, Robert Poste's Child ...
Flora Adam!
Adam   ... I 'ave said too much already ...

  Adam exits

Flora Bother!

Judith groans and lifts her head

Judith Seth, Seth ...
Flora   He's gone out.
Judith Argh! Bring me my album! Bring me my album! If I can't have
  my Seth, I mun at least have his photiegraphs about me!
Flora   Oh, really — this is *too* much. (*She searches about. She sees the
  sukebind and examines it*) Oh ...

  Elfine enters, dancing. She stops dead on seeing Flora

Elfine I be Elfine — you be Flora.
Flora   (*to the audience*) No prizes offered.

Elfine Why be you a'tuggin' at the sukebind?
Flora Oh, so this is the —
Judith Aye — the sukebind! The sukebind! (*She groans and collapses*)
Flora I wonder, would you be a lamb and find your mother's photographs
for me? I must talk with Cousin Reuben.
Elfine Reuben bain't 'ere.

Flora opens a door to reveal Reuben, who is holding a parcel

   Elfine exits

Flora Ah! These will be from Charles.
Reuben Charles?

Laughter offstage from Seth. Judith leaps up

Judith Seth ... (*She runs across the room, making to exit*)
Reuben Mother!

*Reuben rugby tackles Judith. She moans as he throws her over his
shoulder*

Flora Oh, Reuben — you really are the most adorable lamb; underneath
it all, I mean. Over here, please. (*She indicates a chair*)
Reuben (*depositing Judith*) I mun fix our Graceless's leg ...
Flora Thank you. Now, Cousin Judith, about my curtains. They have a
small tear, you see, and I wondered if I might ... Cousin Judith?
Reuben 'Tis useless, Robert Poste's Child. She be out for the ——
Judith (*coming round*) Curtins? Curtins? Child, child, 'tis many years
since such trifles broke across the web of my solitude!
Flora Yes, I'm sure it is — but might I repair them all the same?

Judith collapses

   Oh dear. She's clearly far too busy nursing her grief to even think about
taking up a hem.
Judith (*coming round*) Bisy?! Bisy?! Bisy weaving my own shroud,
belike! But give me time and I will atone. Atone for the wrong my man
once did your father. Give ... us ... all ... time ...

She goes to collapse, but Flora apprehends her

Flora I don't suppose you'd care to tell me what that wrong actually was?
I do think it would make things easier.
Reuben 'Asn't she told you 'er lips are sealed?

Judith does a "my lips are sealed" gesture

Flora Oh, very well. (*She releases Judith*)

Judith collapses

Now then, Cousin Reuben ...

Elfine enters with a photograph album

Elfine 'Ere!
Flora Oh, thank you.
Elfine I write poitry.
Flora Yes, I thought you might.
Judith Seth! (*She stands up and grabs the album*)
Flora Oh!
Judith Look at 'im! Shame of our 'ouse!
Flora (*to the audience*) Two hundred photographs of her son — six weeks
to twenty-four years — decorate the pages of her album. In one of them
he sits — primal king of the Howling Wonders football team. His young
limbs, sleek in their dark male pride, seem almost to disdain their flimsy
coverings. The taut jersey. The straining shorts. His body could be
naked — and might as well be, I suppose. His full, muscled throat rises
from his torso — thrusting, solid, round and proud; like the over-ripe
organ of a yam-yam tree.
Judith Seth ...
Elfine My poems be about Love.
Flora Really?

Elfine dances about

Elfine Love and poetry go together somehow. Out there on the 'ills, when
I be alone wi' my dreams ... Oh, I can't tell 'ee 'ow I feel! I bin chasin'
a marsh-tigget all mornin'!

Flora Very athletic.

She opens a door

  Elfine "falls" out

Flora closes the door

  Sit down please, Cousin.
Judith Cursed be the day as I brought 'im forth! And cursed be the wooing
tongue as he uses upon weak women!
Flora Oh dear, dear, dear. I must see, I think, what can be done about Seth.
(*To the audience*) And it is here that I remember the card he dropped at
breakfast. "Stars of the Silver Screen"?

Judith wails, makes for a door, and opens it

  Elfine runs in, screaming, pursued by Urk. Judith exits

*Reuben rugby tackles Urk. A struggle ensues. Reuben lifts Urk above his
head and makes for a window*

Flora Cousin Reuben!

*Reuben stops, thinks, and then hurls Urk out of the window. We hear Urk's
screech off stage, followed by a thud*

  Would you please put the kettle on? (*To the audience*) The sad and sulky
sun, you see, is sliding slowly, sullenly — alliteratively — down toward
Mock Uncle Hill ——

The Lights change abruptly. Flora produces a book

  — which indicates tea-time. (*She reads from the book*) "Condole with
the Ugly Duckling's mother. She has fathomed the pit of amazement."
Elfine What's that?
Flora *The Higher Common Sense.*
Elfine Eh?
Flora A philosophical treatise, Elfine. An attempt not to explain the
universe — but to reconcile us all to its inexplicability.

Elfine Oh.

Flora (*reading*) "Lost is the man who sees a beautiful woman descending a noble staircase." Hmm ...

Elfine D'you want to 'ear some more o' mun poems?

Flora No, I don't think so. Elfine, are you engaged?

Elfine There do be ... someone. But we don't want to spoil it. 'Tes 'orrible t' bind things down.

Flora Nonsense. It's a very good idea.

Elfine sniffs back a tear

    Elfine?

Elfine It do be Urk!

Flora Urk?

Reuben He means to 'ave 'er for 'is weddin' bed — as soon as 'e's able.

Flora But Urk's surely not the man Elfine *wants* to marry?

Elfine Gran'mother Doom do be sot on it, though — so there bain't no way out! Oh, Cousin Flora ... what am I to do?

Flora We must speak to Cousin Amos.

Reuben Huh! Father doan't want *none* of us to be happy.

Flora Which means, I suppose, that he won't give you the farm?

Elfine Aye! But he doan't give a fig about the land 'imself!

Flora Whilst you, Cousin Reuben, do love each field with the fierce passion of an over-ripe plum — isn't that right?

Reuben Aye ... I loves the land. Even if it do be cursed.

Elfine All Father cares about is misery and sin.

Reuben And the Quivering Brethren!

Flora Quivering Brethren? (*To the audience*) So — he *is* a member of some bizarre religious sect! Excellent! (*To Reuben*) Cousin Reuben — if your father ... went away — the farm would automatically become yours, wouldn't it? I mean, you are the eldest son?

Reuben 'E'll niver go away.

Elfine 'Tes impossible, Cousin Flora.

Flora Oh, I'm sure ——

Reuben Nay, Robert Poste's Child!

Elfine Gran'mother would 'ave an attack!

Flora But if a tractor could be ... An attack?

Elfine Of 'er ...

Reuben 'Er illness.

Flora Illness? But what *is* her illness? Perhaps it could be treated?

Reuben Nay, Robert Poste's Child.

Elfine It can't niver be treated.

Reuben Nor niver cured, neither.

Elfine You see, Cousin Flora, she's ...

Reuben She's ...

Flora Yes?

Ada (*off*) Argh! I saw something Narsty! Narsty, narsty, narsty! I saw something narsty ... in the woodshed!

Reuben Mad.

Flora Mad?

Elfine Aye ...

Flora (*to the audience*) Fat and dark the word hangs between us like a sodden chaff ...

Reuben   }
             (*together*) ... mad!
Elfine   }

Flora Oh.

Elfine And 'tes all part of 'er madness that I must marry Urk — instead o' ... my someone ... (*She weeps*)

Flora Oh, Elfine ...

We hear a dying wail from Ada

Reuben I mun fix our Graceless's leg.

Flora Oh, Cousin Reuben! Your father doesn't *preach* to these Brethren by any chance, I suppose?

Reuben Preach?! He do be speechifyin' at 'em all the time!

Flora Wonderful!

Reuben Eh?

Flora You see, my dear, I don't think the land here is cursed at all — really I don't. (*She opens a door. Calling*) Rennet! (*To Reuben*) It's just your father's terrible mismanagement. Have you a vehicle on the farm?

Reuben Eh?

Flora A tractor, perhaps?

Reuben Father says tractors are the toys o' the Devil.

Flora Yes, he would, I suppose.

Rennet enters. She is wet, and carries a huge yoke on her shoulders with two pails of milk

Oh, my dear — could you be a lamb and attend to Elfine? She's rather upset, you see.

Rennet goes to Elfine and stares at her

Reuben There do be an old tri-cycle, though — with a little platform on the back.
Flora A tri-cycle, though? With a platform on the back? Perfect!
Reuben Not that it goes.
Flora Fiddlesticks!
Reuben But I reckon as I could mend it.
Flora Really?
Reuben It belonged to Mark Dolour, see.

Rennet starts

Flora Mark Dolour?

Rennet starts again

Reuben Aye. But he was always asking *me* to fix it. He weren't no good with 'is 'ands — Mark Dolour.

Rennet exits running, smashing the yoke against the door frame

Flora Oh, dear ... Incidentally, in what way did this Mark Dolour disappoint Rennet — exactly?
Reuben Mark Dolour, he's ... he do be ... he 'as 'is ...
Elfine Problems.
Flora Problems?
Elfine With ...
Reuben With ... Man's Work.
Flora Oh? Well, I'm sure a young woman like myself could do something for him.
Reuben Nay, Robert Poste's Child — young women, yourself or otherwise, mun do nothin' for Mark Dolour at all ...

We hear Rennet screech off stage, followed by a splash

Reuben exits

The kettle whistles

Flora Elfine ...

Elfine removes the kettle from the burner. Flora takes up The Higher Common Sense *and opens the door*

(*Calling*) Rennet! (*Reading*) "Lost is the man who sees a beautiful woman descending a noble staircase." (*To the audience*) Yes, but where will I *find* a staircase?
Elfine Eh?
Flora Still — first things first ... (*She puts the book back in her work-box*) Elfine — about you and this "someone" you want to marry. Does this "someone" know about Urk?
Elfine I did tell him, yes.
Flora And what did he say?
Elfine "Rotten luck, old girl."
Flora It's Richard Hawk-Monitor, isn't it?
Elfine 'Ow did you know?

Flora discovers a spring and a screwdriver in her work-box

Flora Ah! The clock! (*She goes to the clock and begins repairing it*) Isn't it his birthday in April?
Elfine Aye. 'Is mother do be throwin' a ball. Oh, t'would be such fun!
Flora "Diverting", Elfine, or "amusing", but *never* "fun". (*She makes the final adjustment to the clock*) There!

Rennet enters, more wet than before

Rennet — the kettle is boiled and we should like our tea.

Rennet prepares a pot of tea. Flora begins to unwrap her parcel

This ball, Elfine. Where is it to be held?
Elfine In the gardens at Howchicker Hall.
Flora *Hautcouture*, my dove.
Elfine But I woan't be goin'. Gran'mother Doom don't let us accept no invitations — 'less it's to funerals or the churchin' of women.

Flora Don't be silly, Elfine — of course you must go.

Elfine Me? To the ball?!

Flora Of course.

Elfine But 'ow?

Flora By listening carefully to my instructions and obeying each one of them. Do you think you could manage that?

Elfine Oh, Flora! To go to the ball I should do anything you say!

Flora Good. Then you can begin by mending my curtains.

Rennet deposits cups, spoons, etc. on the table. Elfine begins to work on the curtains

(*To the audience*) Poor daft Rennet. What a septic time she has of it. I do wish I could do something for her. (*She holds up a pair of gum-boots from the parcel. To the audience*) And perhaps I can.

Elfine These scissors are a bit blunt.

Flora That's because they're a pair of pliers.

Seth enters, unseen by the others

Rennet begins to pour tea

(*To Rennet*) Now, listen my lamb — about this jumping down the well. Have you ever thought, I wonder, of simply paddling about a bit — instead of going the whole hog, I mean? I'm sure you would find paddling quite as exciting as the full immersion — and far more comfortable. Especially with a pair of these. What size feet do you have?

Rennet smiles and reaches out for the boots, still holding the teapot in her other hand

Seth Rennet!

Elfine Oh!

Seth I've a message for you ... from —

Flora Mark Dolour?

Rennet starts and exits

Seth laughs and goes to move further into the kitchen. Flora holds up her hand and listens. Seth stops. We hear Rennet screech off stage, followed by a splash of water. Flora drops her hand. Seth moves into the kitchen

(*To the audience*) Seth lounges into the kitchen, and brings with him, it seems, the tortured, blood-stained animalism of the dying day.

The clock chimes four o'clock dolefully. The Lights change with the chimes of the clock to a bloodstained-sunset effect. Flora sits with Elfine at the table. Elfine sews as Flora pours tea. Seth prowls about in the bloody shadows and laughs

(*To Elfine*) Tell me, my dove — what colour might you like your ball gown to be?

Elfine Ball gown!

Flora It must, of course, match your shoes.

Elfine Shoes?

Seth What's that she's sewin'?

Flora (*to Seth*) You hope it's a pair of knickers, don't you? Well, it's not. It's a pair of curtains. (*To Elfine*) Yes — shoes.

Elfine Oh, I could niver wear no shoes, Cousin Flora! Not if I'm to walk all down that staircase.

Seth Huh! Sewin'!

Flora Nonsense. Elegant shoes are vital to — Staircase?

Seth Women's nonsense!

Flora What staircase?

Elfine At Howchicker 'All. The grand staircase — leadin' down on to the lawn ...

Flora Oh, my lamb! The gods — and Common Sense — have smiled on us, indeed!

Elfine Eh?

Seth Aye, you're all alike — women. A-fussin' over your fal-la-lals and bedazzlin' in a man's eyes — when all you really want is the 'eart out of 'is body, an' 'is soul, an' 'is pride!

Flora (*to Seth*) Really? (*To Elfine*) More tea, my lamb?

Seth And when you've got 'im all bound up in your priddy ways and your softness, and 'e can't get out because of the longin' for you as cries out in 'is man's blood — d'you know what you do to 'im then?!

Flora (*to Seth*) I'm afraid not. (*To Elfine*) But be warned, Elfine; if you *are* to marry Richard Hawk-Monitor ——

Elfine Marry?! Richard?!

Seth You eats 'im! Like an 'en-spider eats a cock-spider!

Flora — you must become accomplished in all the arts and graces expected of a young woman.

Seth That's what women do — if a man lets 'em!

Flora (*to Seth*) Indeed? (*To Elfine*) Have you, Elfine, the stomach for such instruction?

Elfine Oh, Flora!

Seth But only if a man lets 'em, I said!

The two women look at Seth

And I don't!

Flora Don't you?

Seth No. (*Pause*) 'Cause I eats them instead!

Flora Oh.

Seth That shocks you, dunnit?

Flora Yes, I think it's dreadful. (*To Elfine*) Have you finished those, my pet?

Seth Dreadful?

Flora Then run along upstairs with them.

Elfine But Flora —

Flora Elfine — run along upstairs.

Elfine exits with the curtains

Seth prowls about. Flora packs her things away into her work-box

Seth Dreadful? Huh! I'll lay you haven't understood the half o' what I been sayin'.

Flora I'm afraid I wasn't even listening to most of it. And really I don't think it was interesting *you* very much either, was it?

Seth Eh?

Flora Now then, Cousin Seth — let's talk about what *does* interest you, shall we?

Seth We was.

Flora Oh, no. You don't really want to eat women at all, do you? No. You'd far sooner admire them. On the silver screen. (*She produces the card which Seth dropped earlier in the scene*) Miss Funchal. You dropped her at breakfast. Have you a big collection?

Seth Fifteen o' Lotta Funchal. Forty o' Jenny Carrol, fifty-five o' Laura

Vallee, twenty o' Caroline Heavytree. Oh, and seventy-four o' Sigrid
Maelstrom. Signed ones.

Flora And all of them actresses? Quite. Because that's your *real* passion
— isn't it, Cousin Seth? The cinema.

Pause

Seth Aye — 'tes truth. I loves the talkies. Many's the girl as I won't niver
see again — 'cause she 'ave worried me in the middle of a picture. They
must 'ave all of you — see? Ivery bit o' your time and thoughts. But I'm
not like that. I just like the talkies.

Flora Better than mollocking?

Seth Aye — much bedder nor mollocking! Bedder nor mother, bedder nor
this farm — bedder nor anythin' in the whoal world ...

Flora Oh, Seth ... Seth! I don't suppose — now I know this might sound
ridiculous — but, I don't suppose you can waltz by any chance, can you?

Seth Course I can waltz!

Flora Really?

Seth Course! I learnt it watching Lotta Funchal's last film — *Back, Side,
Together.*

Flora Splendid! And you will, I'm sure, look wonderful in a tuxedo.

Seth Tuxedo?

Flora Cousin Seth — I want you to come to a ball with myself and Elfine.
There'll be somebody there whom I really think you should meet.

There is a thud upstairs from Ada and a terrible wail. Seth makes to exit

Cousin Seth?

Another thud from upstairs. Ada wails. The clock explodes

Seth exits

Oh dear. (*She takes the pliers from her work-box, goes to the clock and
begins to fix it*)

SCENE 5

*The kitchen and Ada's room above. This entire scene is delivered with
each character addressing the audience*

Flora Still, apart from my "rights", this clock, and the mystery of the "wrong", I really think I'm progressing quite well, don't you? (*She finishes working on the clock*) There! (*She fetches a candle [this is a battery operated, "flickering flame"-like bulb]*) And this, only the end of my first day. (*She switches on the candle*)

A pale pool of Light flickers around Flora. The clock begins to chime midnight. During the following the Lights dim further as the chimes continue, dolefully

I have discovered that Cousin Judith's fixation is her own son, Cousin Seth — and that Cousin Seth's interests lie more in the picture palace than in mollocking. Cousin Amos turns out to be a susceptible evangelist and Cousin Reuben a co-operative darling. Elfine, the poetic dryad, is well on the way to recovery and when dressed in a ball gown will be transformed, I am sure, into a quite normal and attractive young woman. I have advised Adam on the merits of a little mop and effected a very neat and almost invisible repair on my curtains. Tomorrow Rennet shall wash them for me — equipped with gum-boots. Indeed, so exhausted am I by my prodigious labours that I should like nothing more than to retire to my room and rest my exhausted head upon my cool pillow. But this luxury I cannot yet allow myself, for the problem of Aunt Ada remains outstanding — and I must not even contemplate sleep until I have given Doom at least a little thought. (*She takes* The Higher Common Sense *from her work-box*) "*The Higher Common Sense*". (*She sits at the table, draws the candle to her, and reads*) "Chapter One — An All-Inclusive Outline".

The clock chimes twelve, and the Lights fade almost entirely. A shaft of chilly moonlight catches the clock and falls across the sukebind. There is an eerie wind. The clock ticks deeply, rhythmically, slowly. Flora, reading, is isolated in a pool of candlelight. Shadowy Lights come up on Ada

Ada I, Ada Doom, am included in no outline! I am alone — upstairs. I sit upstairs — alone. I am the matrix, the focusing-point, the core of it all. And like all cores — an apple core — or a pear core, even — I am utterly and irrevocably — alone. Alone I am, and irrevocable is the utterness of it. Yet, in the loneliness of my utter — which is irrevocable — all the

wandering waves of desire, passion, jealousy and lust, that throb
through this house like a steel thread, converge, web-like, upon my core
solitude. I feel myself to be a core, a matrix, a focusing-point ... And
utterly, irrevocably — alone! (*She takes a huge breath and exhales*)

*A wind moves through the kitchen. Doors rattle. Windows bang. Flora's
candle gutters a little*

I will not see my niece! I will not see Robert Poste's Child! When I was
very small, so small that the lightest puff of wind did blow my little
crinoline over the top of my head, I saw something ... narsty ... in the
woodshed! And ever since that day my very thoughts have been beasts
to me — so I have run away. Away from the huge and terrifying world!
I have shut myself up in this room — where my beast-thoughts rub
themselves against the dumb walls like drowsy yaks. Yes! Yaks!
Exactly like yaks! Outside things can happen — but nothing can happen
here. And none of my family might leave me! (*She thrusts a hand,
graspingly, into the air*)

*With a bizarre, tortured, squeaking creak, the sukebind begins to move.
There is more creaking, and the pressure on the sacking increases. The
ropes snap, the padlock and chains shatter and, with a mighty, rendering
thrust, the sukebind bursts forth. Thick tendrils spiral slowly toward the
ceiling; others twist about the beams; a few simply hang in the air, or
slither across the floor. As the Starkadders enter they are each caught by
the tendrils of the sukebind and become entwined as a group by the plant*

Judith ——

Judith appears in the kitchen below

Judith ⎫
Ada   ⎬ (*together*) — might not leave.
Ada Amos ——

Amos appears in the kitchen

Amos ⎫
Judith ⎬ (*together*) — might not leave.
Ada   ⎭

Ada Urk ——

Urk appears in the kitchen

Urk
Amos
Judith   } *(together)* — might not leave.
Ada

Ada Elfine ——

Elfine appears in the kitchen

Elfine
Urk
Amos   } *(together)* — might not leave.
Judith
Ada

Ada Reuben ——

Reuben appears in the kitchen

Reuben
Elfine
Urk
Amos   } *(together)* — might not leave.
Judith
Ada

Ada And most of all — Seth ——

Seth appears in the kitchen

Seth
Reuben
Elfine
Urk   } *(together)* — might not leave.
Amos
Judith
Ada

The Starkadders are now grouped in the kitchen between Flora, at her book, and Ada, in her room. They form a human barricade dividing the two women

Ada I have them all ——
Starkadders All!
Ada — in the twisted, writhen fingers of my age-old hand! (*She takes another deep breath*)

The wind again moves through the kitchen. As it touches the Starkadders they take a collective breath. The Starkadders and Ada hold their breath for a moment. Flora looks around as if she's heard something, then returns to her book. Ada exhales, with a shudder

   Argh ...

The Starkadders exhale

Starkadders Argh ...
Ada Oh ...
Starkadders Oh ...
Ada
            (*together*) How like yaks are these drowsy thoughts!
Starkadders
Ada I sit here——
Ada
            (*together*) — alone,
Starkadders
Ada living from meal to meal. Monday ——
Starkadders — pork.
Ada Tuesday ——
Starkadders — beef.
Ada Wednesday ——
Starkadders — mutton.
Ada Thursday ——
Starkadders — veal.
Ada Friday ——
Starkadders — stew.
Ada Saturday ——
Starkadders — toad-in-the-hole with a little bit of cabbage — or perhaps mashed swede as she prefers — followed by bruised-apple dumplings

and a small crocket of cream; if so be as our Graceless is up to it that
week.
Ada Sunday ——
Starkadders — chops.

Pause

Ada I — am — mad!
Starkadders Mad!
Ada The woodshed incident, all those years ago, did twist something in
my child-brain. And seeing it's because of that incident that I sit here,
alone, ruling the roost and having five meals a day brought up to me as
regular as clockwork, it wasn't such a bad break for me, was it? That day,
all them years ago, that day, when I was only a child, that day
when I ——

Judith ⎫
         ⎬ *(together)* — saw ——
Ada ⎭

Amos ⎫
Judith ⎬ *(together)* — something ——
Ada ⎭

Reuben ⎫
Amos ⎪
       ⎬ *(together)* — narsty ——
Judith ⎪
Ada ⎭

Starkadders ⎫
         ⎬ *(together)* in the woodshed!
Ada ⎭

Pause. The clock explodes. Black-out, including Flora's candle

The Starkadders and Ada exit

Spotlight up on Flora

Flora No, that's not the interval, I'm afraid. Just a few more scenes in the
kitchen, a nice little moment with the Quivering Brethren, and then you
can all have a drink. All right? Good.

The Lights come up a little

The Chorus enters

It is now the end of April. The swedes have been gathered — the beet harvest not yet begun ...

SCENE 6

The kitchen

Flora (*to the audience*) ... and I am really quite enjoying myself! Oh, dear ... (*She goes to the clock and begins repairing it*)
Chorus The hot juice of reproduction rises in the loins of all living things. Worm jars with worm and seed with seed. Frond leaps on root. Pea-bug and flinch-fly are neither spared. Eek moths, locked in a blind embrace, spin radiantly through the glutinous haze to their pre-ordained deaths. The deranged to-wit to-woos of nocturnal owls echo, unnaturally, through daylight skies — scarlet shrieks 'gainst livid silver. In the pauses, every ten minutes, the female lays an egg.
Flora (*finishing repairing the clock*) Which is just as well, really; it is, after all — spring.

Flora and the Chorus exit

The clock explodes. The Lights come up to a fecund-spring-day effect. We hear the twittering of birds, the bleating of sheep, etc.

Adam and Rennet enter. Rennet wears gum-boots and is dry. She has done something enterprising with her hair and clothes. Adam has sukebind-tidying equipment. He and Rennet begin fixing the sukebind to beams, etc.

Reuben enters. He wears greasy overalls and carries a tricycle wheel and a parcel

Reuben If them buds do open they'll surely stink the place out.
Adam There be no "if" about it ...
Reuben Bain't no stench so sickly in the whoarl'.
Adam ... 'tes the sukebind!
Reuben Cousin Flora won't like it.

Adam Robert Poste's Child ... Huh! 'Er does nothin' but meddle — and put ideas in folkses 'eads.

Reuben puts down the wheel and offers Adam the parcel

Reuben A parcel for 'ee.
Adam I niver get no parcels.
Reuben You 'ave this mornin'.
Adam Postman 'asn't bin yet.
Reuben It didn't come by post. 'Twas sent by van from a shop — in Lunnon.

Adam opens the parcel and takes out a dish mop with a red ribbon attached to the handle

Adam A liddle mop? For me? Why, 'tes priddier ... 'tes priddier nor anything ... and 'tes mine, you say?
Reuben Aye.
Adam Oh! Nor house nor kine, and yet 'tes mine!
Reuben So now 'ee can wash the dishes proper, can't 'ee? See. Cousin Flora be not all bad, do she?
Adam Robert Poste's Child?
Reuben She sent for it — remember?
Adam Nay, I mun niver put this dainty head in no greasy washin' up water! Why, 'tes priddier nor apple blooth, my liddle mop!

Rennet and Adam dance. Rennet remains mute while Adam carries on, "My liddle mop", etc.

Amos enters with Judith behind him

Judith Amos!
Amos Where be my warmin' ...?

Adam and Rennet stop dead. Amos stares at them, takes the warming-pan and brandishes it at them

Devil creatures! (*He makes to exit*)
Judith No! Not now!
Amos I mun go whensoe're the Lord calls me to it!

Reuben But there's beets to be gathered on Mock Uncle Hill!

Amos And souls to be gathered on the village green!

Judith Cannot you leave the brethren to quiver without 'ee for once?

Amos Leave the Quiverin' Brethren? What? So as Deborah Checkbottom might get up and preach?

Reuben She'd speechified before!

Amos That was a mistake! The Devil's way is dark — and the spirit as was sent by the Lord for me, was guided, by the Devil, into Deborah Checkbottom!

Reuben Aye! An' 'ow did 'ee lit the Devil out?

Judith Reuben!

Reuben 'Ee did strike poor Deborah down wi' 'is gurt old warmin' pan — that's 'ow!

Amos Aye! An' the Devil came out of 'er, din' he? We've heard no more o' Deborah tryin' to preach!

Reuben We've heard no more o' Deborah 'cause she's dead!

Judith Reuben!

Amos Enough! (*He strikes the table violently with the warming-pan*)

Silence and stillness for a moment. Amos glares at everybody in the room

Reuben, Adam, Rennet and Judith exit one by one

Amos sees the dangling sukebind. He lifts the warming-pan and strikes at the sukebind, wildly but ineffectually. He goes to the cupboard, takes out a black hat and coat and puts them on

He makes a last assault on the sukebind and exits. Flora and Elfine enter. Flora wears a summer outfit. Elfine is reasonably clean and wears an embroidered smock

Flora You see, my dove — if one *encourages* people to be messy, they will *be* messy. (*She sees the clock*) Oh, not again ... (*She goes to the clock and begins repairing it*)

Elfine But when you '*ave* tidied up Seth ——

Flora *And* Cousin Judith ...

Elfine — will that mean you'll be leavin' us, then?

Flora Oh no ... (*finishing with the clock*) There! No, Elfine — my campaign at Cold Comfort Farm will be terminated only by the abrupt appearance of some poor soul carrying an old-fashioned camera, a tripod and a flash lamp.

Elfine Eh?

Flora (*to the audience*) This will, of course, signal a "Let's-Pretend-To-Be-A-Photograph"-type effect. And once a "Let's-Pretend-To-Be-A-Photograph"-type effect has been arrived at in a Theatrical Adaptation of a Classic Rural Novel then the end of the whole hysterical affair cannot be far behind — can it? (*To Elfine*) Now — about your hair. We must have it styled in London, of course.

Elfine Lunnon?!

Flora We shall go up tomorrow.

Elfine Oh!

Flora I should like to leave earlier, of course — but the invitations might arrive in my absence and fall into the wrong hands.

Elfine Oh, the ball! The ball. (*She dances about*)

Flora (*to the audience*) Mind you, invitations to balls nearly always arrive in the Heroine's absence and never fail to fall into the wrong hands — so we'll just have to lump it, I suppose. (*To Elfine*) Elfine!

Elfine stops dancing

We must not let excitement distract us from our purpose. You have studied well, my dove, since first we met; and have marshalled your body into a measure of restraint. Your psyche, however, is not yet of the kind that could ever be tolerated in the wife of an English aristocrat.

Elfine Then what's to be done?

Flora Your artiness must be rooted out — entirely. You must forget all poetry, deny your affinity with St Francis of Assisi — and wear no more smocks. You must be long-limbed, clear-eyed — and inhibited. The first two qualities you have always possessed — the last you have yet to acquire.

Elfine But can't I keep just one nice smock?

Flora There is no such thing as a "nice smock". Truly graceful design depends upon a pure line and a delicate weave. All gross and embroidered romanticism must be purged away revealing uncorrupted art in only a fold or a flute. It is this pared delicacy that you will find in the style of Miss Austen and the pages of *Vogue* — and it is this kind of beauty, Elfine, that you must learn to look for in your everyday life. This is Knowledge! And you must on no account be frightened of it.

Elfine Oh, I'm not! No, the only thing as scares me now is The Countin' ...

Flora Yes, what is this Counting?

Elfine 'Tes when Gran'mother gathers us all in — and counts us.

Flora *All*? You mean there are *more* of you?

Elfine Oh, *lots*! Nephews, aunts, wives and cousins ... But we niver see each other, really — 'ceptin once a year. At The Countin' ...

Flora And that's when this sukebind opens, I suppose, and all the trouble begins?

Elfine Aye — 'tes terrible ... Oh! The postman! (*She rushes to the door*)

Urk enters with a large, gold-trimmed envelope

Ah!

Urk Ha! And what's in this liddle envelopey, I wonder? Aye — you do think you're smart, doan't 'ee? Think I doan't know what's goin' on — wi' your invites from 'Owchicker 'All. Ha! Now, listen to me! She'm mine, I tell 'ee! She'm ...

Flora Yours — yes, I heard you the first time. Now, would you please give me my letter?

Urk Ledder? What ledder? Ha! I doan't see no ledder! I only sees a bit o' kindlin'. A bit o' kindlin' — for the fire ... (*He moves toward the fire, passing the clock*)

Elfine Oh, Flora, Flora ...!

The clock explodes, knocking Urk, unconscious, to the ground. Flora snatches the envelope from his hand and pats the clock

Flora And lump it we did!

Urk moans and begins to get up

Elfine Flora!

Flora Quickly Elfine, we must leave for London ——

Urk 'Ere!

Flora (*snatching up the wheel*) — at once!

Urk Elfine !

Flora and Elfine exit, pursued by Urk

SCENE 7

The meeting place of the Quivering Brethren. The sole piece of furniture is a bizarre piano/pulpit affair

Amos enters with his warming-pan. He plays a hymn. The Quivering Brethren enter and sing in dirge-like fashion

Brethren (*singing*) Whatever shall we do, O Lord,
When wretches in vainglorious pride
Do burn and perish in accord
With God, for sins he'll not abide?

We know what we must do, O Lord,
When Gabriel blows o'er sea and river,
Fen and desert, mount and ford.
The earth may burn, but we will quiver.

Amos climbs into the pulpit with his warming pan. His following sermon is punctuated by industrious quivering and wailing from the Brethren

Amos (*to the audience*) So — 'ave ye come? Old 'n' young, sick 'n' well, matrons 'n' virgins — to 'ear me tellin' o' the gurt, crimson-lickin' flames o' hell fire? Aye, ye've come. But what good will it do 'ee? Nowt! Not a flicker nor a whisper of a bit o' good. Ye're all damned! Damned! Oh, do ye ever stop to think what that word means? Nay! Well, I'll tell 'ee. It means endless 'orrifyin' torment, wi' your poor sinful bodies stretched out on red 'ot gridirons in the nethermost pit of hell! 'Ee knows, doan't 'ee, 'ow it feels when 'ee burns yer hand in takin' a cakie out o' the oven? Aye. It stings wi' a fearful pain, doan't it? And 'ee do clap a bit o' butter on to take the pain away. Aye — but 'till not be like that in hell. Nay! In hell yer whoal body'll be burnin' and stingin' wi' that unbearable pain! Yer blackened tongues'll be stickin' out of yer mouth, and yer cracked and parchy lips'll try an' scream out for a drop o' water, but no sound woan't come out! Nay! 'Cause yer throat'll be drier nor the sandy desert! And yer eyes'll be beatin' like red-hot globes against their shrivelled lids! And your twisted 'and'll reach out for that merciful butter-pat! Aye, reach out it will, reach out in all its agony. But yer dunnay bother to reach out in hell. Yer dunnay bother to reach out for that butter-pat. For in hell — there be no butter!

The Brethren wail. There is the sound of a tricycle bell off stage

Flora and Elfine enter on a tricycle: Elfine pedalling, Flora Boadicea-like on a platform

Flora Cousin Amos?
Amos Robert Poste's Child!
Flora Do you think you could move these people along, please? We're in rather a hurry, you see.
Amos I be preachin'! I mun prepare them for their torment!

Flora climbs down from the tricycle

Urk appears, some way off

Urk Ah!
Elfine Flora ...
Flora One moment, Elfine!
Elfine But ...!
Flora Is this your entire congregation?
Amos Why?
Flora Oh no, it's splendid — in a humble sort of way. But you know, Cousin Amos, there's a terribly big, and really very sinful world outside the village. I'm surprised you've never thought about ... touring.
Amos 'Bout what?
Flora Touring! Touring the country on a nice old tricycle — just like this one! A nice old tricycle with a little platform on the back? Preaching on market days, and spreading The Word up and down the country!

The Brethren murmur amongst themselves

And you could take the Brethren with you! I'm sure they would enjoy singing to a larger audience — wouldn't you, my lovelies?
Amos 'Ere!

Flora climbs on to the tricycle platform

Flora (*to the Brethren*) It's quite comfortable, you see. And if you were to stand on the back, like this, you wouldn't have to worry at all about the crowds not seeing you.

Brethren Crowds?

Flora Aye! Multitudes!

The Brethren squeal and quiver with delight. They crowd in closer around Flora

Amos Nay! 'Twould be puffin' ourselves up! 'Twould be thinkin' of our own miserable glory — instead o' the glory o' the Lord!

The Brethren murmur assent and shuffle back toward Amos

Flora But Brothers! That is surely putting your own wicked souls before the souls of everyone else? One must be prepared, I think, to sin oneself in order to save others!

A mumble of confusion from the Brethren

At least, that is what *I* should be prepared to do — if I were unfortunate enough to be called upon by the Lord to go preaching around the country on a nice old tricycle with a little platform on the back so that the multitudes could see me!

Excitement from the Brethren. They move back toward Flora

Amos Nay, it be a test! A test of our souls! A test of our Godliness!

The Brethren stop dead

Brethren Ah, Godliness ... Ah, Godliness ...

Amos For how do we know that it be the Lord that calls us — and not the Devil dressed up to deceive!

The Brethren quiver and move back toward Amos

Brethren Ah, deceive ... Ah, deceive ...

Flora But what does it matter who it is that calls you, so long as you save souls?

The Brethren quiver once more and move back toward Flora

Brethren Ah, souls ... Ah, souls ...
Amos Don't listen to 'er! Don't listen to 'er!

Urk appears, closer now

Urk Ah!
Elfine Flora! Please!
Flora Goodness!

The Brethren begin to chant rhythmically

Brethren Nice old tricycle — with platform on the back! Nice old tricycle
— with platform on the back!

*They continue chanting as Amos leaps down from the pulpit and moves
among the Brethren, clutching at them*

Amos Nay, nay! *I* am your saviour! It's *me* you mun follow!

*At this point Amos passes in front of Urk, who grabs Amos and hurls him
aside*

Urk Ah!
Amos Argh!
Flora Brothers! Brothers! Fear not! I shall return! And I shall bring the
tricycle with me!

The Brethren cheer. Urk fights past them, making for the tricycle

Urk Ah!
Flora Quickly, Elfine! Quickly!

Elfine and Flora pedal off

*The ecstatic Brethren start to follow. Urk gives chase to them all. Amos
leaps up with a cry and brandishes his warming-pan*

Amos You're all damned! Damned!

The Brethren turn back, and with a wild cry of dissent they charge on Amos. Urk leaps back as the Brethren thunder past

Amos exits, terrified. The Brethren chase off after him

Silence. Urk staggers forward and looks off after Elfine and Flora

Urk E-l-f-i-n-e!

Silence

With a great wail the Brethren now thunder back on, with Amos held high above them. The Brethren trample Urk to the ground and exit

Silence and stillness for a moment. There is a great, pained wail from Amos and an offstage whoop of glee from the Brethren. The whooping slowly fades away

Amos staggers back on in tatters. His warming-pan, buckled and broken, is wrapped about him somehow

A flattened Urk lifts his head and peers at Amos

Urk Elfine ...?
Amos Oh ... Shut up!

Amos strikes Urk on head with the warming-pan. Urk shrieks and collapses

Black-out

CURTAIN

ACT II

SCENE 1

The gardens at Hautcouture Hall. The evening of the ball

As the CURTAIN *rises we hear gentle waltz music. A great staircase dominates the gardens, which are peppered with chinese lanterns*

Richard and Mrs Hawk-Monitor stand chatting at the bottom of the stairs. Sneller is calling out the names of the guests as they appear. They are greeted warmly by Mrs Hawk-Monitor and Richard

Sneller Miss Cavendish and Mr Arndale. Dame Ely and Lord Castleford of Cranbrook. Lady Smollet and Viscount Philpot of Argyle. Miss Lymington and Miss Boundy. Miss Norris and her brother, Sir George Hustible. Lady Jopling of Bath and her niece, Miss Block.

The waltz ends. Applause. The guests mill about, chatting happily. Sneller distributes drinks

Neck enters

Neck Hey, Catherine! You're looking great! And Dicky! How's tricks? Gee, but I'm sorry I'm late!

Mrs Hawk-Monitor But what on earth were you *doing* in France, Mr Neck?

Neck Looking for an actor. But ... didn't find him. Not in France — not nowhere. Has my pal arrived yet?

Mrs Hawk-Monitor Pal?

Neck Miss Poste.

Mrs Hawk-Monitor Who?

Richard I'm dreadfully sorry, Mother, but you see ... I invited her.

Mrs Hawk-Monitor I beg your pardon?

Richard And the Starkadders.

Mrs Hawk-Monitor Starkadders? What Starkadders?
Neck All my doing, Mrs H. Flora's a buddy of mine.
Mrs Hawk-Monitor Flora?
Neck You see, she'd heard such terrific things about these beautiful
  gardens — and the beautiful hostess.
Mrs Hawk-Monitor Oh. Oh well, if they're friends of yours, Mr Neck,
  I shall tell Sneller to make them welcome. Sneller!

Mrs Hawk-Monitor exits

Richard Thanks awfully, Earl.
Neck So what's the problem, here?
Richard Elf.
Neck Elf?
Richard Sorry. Pet name. Elfine.
Neck You said you were stuck on the broad!
Richard Oh, I am. Like a limpet. It's just that ... well — she *is* rather
  peculiar. Not at all the sort that Mother would approve of.
Neck I get it.
Richard And to top it all she's bringing her brother — Seth.
Neck Seth?
Richard 'Fraid so. I shudder to think what *he'll* be like. Probably spend
  most of his time eating the champagne glasses. Oh, Earl — how frightful
  this all is!

Mrs Hawk-Monitor enters

Mrs Hawk-Monitor Well, they've arrived! The ladies are in the
  cloakroom, repairing their faces, but *Mr* Starkadder is on his way now!
Richard Ah ...
Mrs Hawk-Monitor Oh, why didn't you tell me about him, Richard?
Richard I had meant to warn you, but ...
Mrs Hawk-Monitor What an extraordinary creature he is! Quite delight-
  ful!
Neck Delightful?
Mrs Hawk-Monitor Oh not, perhaps, to a gentleman's eyes — but to we
  gels ... Body-thrilling! Oh! Here he comes, now! (*She moves away*)
Richard Earl?
Neck Listen, Dicky — I'll deal with Seth — you just keep this Elfine dame
  out of sight, OK?

Richard K.O.
Sneller Mr Seth Starkadder — of Howling.

Seth enters. He wears a tuxedo and his hair is slicked back. He looks stunning

Mrs Hawk-Monitor Hello there, Mr Starkadder! Jolly glad you could make it! I am Mrs Hawk-Monitor — Richard's mother. I feel I have to point that out; I'm so often, you see, taken for his sister, ha ha! My husband, I am sorry to say, died some time ago. Which means, of course, Mr Starkadder, that I am a widow ... some would say of the "merry" variety, ha ha!

Seth takes her hand, kisses it, and bows gracefully

Seth 'Ow kind of you to let me come.

A gasp from the guests. Mrs Hawk-Monitor nearly passes out. Dance music begins. Seth looks about the guests. The men eye him with suspicion, while the women giggle and chatter excitedly. Seth walks about slowly, looking at the women. After a brief pause he moves to Mrs Hawk-Monitor and holds out his hand. There is a gasp from the crowd. Seth leads Mrs Hawk-Monitor to the centre of the lawn and they begin to dance. Seth is a quite beautiful dancer. The guests look on, reacting variously. Mrs Hawk-Monitor now apprehends their dancing for a moment, indicating that she is a little fatigued, and gestures for one of the other women to come forward. Seth and his new partner now dance about the lawn, while Mrs Hawk-Monitor withdraws to Mr Neck's side and looks on happily. A short but graceful sequence follows in which various ladies "excuse me", and dance with Seth one after another. As each woman leaves Seth, she takes the arm of one of the male guests and leads him on to the lawn. This is all quite smooth, and formally orchestrated. There should be a feeling of the lawn being gradually filled with delighted guests

Mrs Hawk-Monitor Oh, what a charmer he is!
Neck You're telling me!

Mrs Hawk-Monitor crooks her arm as an invitation to dance

Mrs Hawk-Monitor Mr Neck ...?

Neck Not now, honey — I gotta make a call.
Mrs Hawk-Monitor A call?
Neck Sure. To Hollywood!

Neck exits

Mrs Hawk-Monitor Oh ...

Richard approaches

Richard Mother?
Mrs Hawk-Monitor Ah ...!

Suddenly, as one, Richard and his mother sweep into the dance. The whole lawn is now a swirling mass of movement, colour and elegance. The dancing continues

Flora appears at the bottom of the stairs with Sneller close by. She wears a simple but fetching dress. She talks closely with Sneller

Flora (*to the audience*) I have worked hard, as you can see, *not* to look beautiful. I would have it no other way. *This* evening is *Elfine's* evening. I know that I look distinguished, elegant and interesting. I ask for nothing more.

The music ends and the guests applaud graciously

Sneller Ladies and Gentlemen ...

A hush falls. Pause

Miss Elfine Starkadder.

Everyone remains motionless, looking up

Elfine appears at the top of the stairs. She is dressed in the most beautiful gown. Her hair has been cut and styled in a remarkably becoming fashion

There is a gasp of appreciation from the audience, perhaps even a little applause, and then a return to expectant silence. Richard now moves, astonished, to the bottom of the stairs. Everyone else remains stationary

Richard Elfine?

Elfine looks down at him and smiles. She glides slowly, extremely slowly, down the staircase. Everyone follows her closely with their eyes. Elfine reaches the foot of the stairs

Flora "Lost is the man who sees a beautiful woman descending a noble staircase"!

Richard holds out his hand

Richard Elfine?

Pause. Elfine takes Richard's hand. Richard goes down on one knee. Some of the guests now edge towards Richard and Elfine, but Flora swiftly intercedes and guides them back on to the lawn. There is a buzz of delighted chatter

Neck enters and moves to Flora

Neck and Flora are now some way from Richard and Elfine, but the audience can see Elfine and Richard talking closely

Neck Flora, honey! I've been looking for you everywhere!
Flora I have been busy, Mr Neck — with my protegée.
Neck Yeah, yeah, she's beautiful.
Flora Thank you.
Neck But not nearly so beautiful as the guy!
Flora Cousin Seth? Yes, I hoped you might be impressed. Easy on the eye, yet conveniently slow on the uptake.
Neck You don't think he'll be difficult, then? I mean, what if he doesn't *want* to be a film star?
Flora Oh! Mr Neck ...

Richard mounts the staircase

Richard Ladies and Gentlemen ...
Flora Ah! He must announce it now! He *must*!
Neck Announce what?
Richard The evening is drawing to a close, but before you all leave I have a jolly important announcement to make! I'm sure I don't have to say just what a top-hole affair this party has been — largely due to the scrummy nature of all you guests. But there is one person here tonight who really is quite wizzingly spiffing — Miss Elfine Starkadder ...

Elfine joins Richard

Most of you, tonight, will meet this young lady, I hope. If, however, by some rotten bad luck you don't, let me assure you that you will certainly have the opportunity of doing so in the very near future. For whenever you visit Hautcouture Hall again, which I jolly well hope will be soon, you will be entertained not only by myself — but by my charming and, I'm sure you will agree, jolly beautiful wife!

A delighted gasp from the guests

Yes ... Miss Starkadder and I are engaged to be married!

Richard and Elfine embrace and kiss. There is applause and cheering from the guests. The couple now come down the stairs and make for Flora

The guests begin to drift off. Throughout the following they eventually disappear altogether

Neck (*seeing Seth off stage; calling*) Hey, Seth!

Neck strides off

Elfine Flora, this is Richard!
Flora How do you do.
Richard Jolly glad to meet you, Miss Poste. Elf has told me so much —
Elfine "Elfine", Richard, or "My Dearest" — but *never* "Elf". I am not a marsh tigget — nor even a pharisee of the woods; isn't that so, Cousin Flora?

Flora Quite so, Cousin Elfine.

Richard Sorry. Mind you, however I introduce you to mother, it'll not make much difference.

Flora Would you like me to speak to her?

Elfine Oh, would you, Flora?

Mrs Hawk-Monitor enters

Mrs Hawk-Monitor Richard!

Richard Lummey ...

Flora Run along now, both of you — it's all going to be fine.

Mrs Hawk-Monitor Richard!

Elfine Oh, thank you, Flora — thank you so much!

Elfine and Richard exit

Flora (*to the audience*) Now this could be tricky. She might be a darling and an absolute love, but she is also, one must remember, a mother ...

Mrs Hawk-Monitor approaches

How do you do, Mrs Hawk-Monitor? I am Miss Poste — Miss Starkadder's companion. Such a lovely party. So kind of you to invite us. And what a happy way to end it all — don't you think?

Mrs Hawk-Monitor Miss Poste, I will be frank with you. I cannot pretend to be delighted at this engagement. Miss Starkadder seems attractive enough in herself — but who exactly is she? And what, more to the point, of her family?

Flora My dear Mrs Hawk-Monitor — one need only look into your beguiling eyes to see that you are neither resentful nor narrow-minded.

Mrs Hawk-Monitor Well ... I hope that I am not.

Flora But naturally you are concerned for your son — as any truly affectionate mother must be.

Mrs Hawk-Monitor Oh, Miss Poste — you read me like a book ...

Flora Miss Starkadder is a gentle, docile person. I'm sure she can be moulded in whatever way you choose. As for her relations — well, yes ... the Starkadders *are* a very old and established family; I fear there may be opposition to the match.

Mrs Hawk-Monitor Opposition? Gracious — they should overjoyed at their offspring's luck!

Flora Indeed. But the grandmother, you see, is most protective of Elfine, and has always intended she should marry ... well, someone else.

Mrs Hawk-Monitor Someone else?

Flora It is Elfine's parents, however, that must give their consent. Elfine, you understand, is not yet twenty-one. Amos and Judith, I am sure, will be no trouble at all — whilst Mrs Doom ——

Mrs Hawk-Monitor Doom?!

Flora — the grandmother — has no legal hold over Elfine at all. I think it is best, however, to err on the side of caution. I recommend a wedding as soon as possible. This will both impress the Starkadders and rob Mrs Doom of any opportunity to object.

Mrs Hawk-Monitor Oh dear ... I was hoping for a year's engagement at least. Richard is still so very young.

Flora Then he should begin at once to be utterly happy.

Mrs Hawk-Monitor But oh, what names! "Starkadder" and "Doom"! So ageing and putting off ...

Music drifts faintly across the lawn

You, however, Miss Poste, are clearly a young woman of great insight as far as character is concerned, and of the most persuasive acumen with regard to social conduct. Sneller!

Sneller enters

Sneller Madam?

Mrs Hawk-Monitor Come with me at once. We must draw up a seating plan for the wedding!

Sneller Wedding?

Mrs Hawk-Monitor Be sure to turn off the lanterns ... Oh, and do tell the orchestra that the ball is over!

Mrs Hawk-Monitor exits followed by Sneller

Pause. Flora walks about a little. Chinese lanterns go off, cluster by cluster, until the lawn is washed only by the pale moonlight. The music fades

Flora (*to the audience*) What a curious evening this has been for me. I have experienced the thrill of seeing Elfine engaged, and the satisfaction of allying Cousin Seth to Mr Neck. Yet I find myself now — strangely melancholy ... (*She looks up into the night sky*)

There is a gentle twinkle of shimmering stars

Charles ... Oh, Charles! In a tail coat of darkest blue!

Seth enters, wearing a coat and carrying Elfine's and Flora's coats

Seth It's time we was leavin' ...

Elfine enters

Elfine Flora! Mrs Hawk-Monitor has agreed to the wedding! She wants it as soon as possible!
Flora Well done, Elfine!
Seth Huh! Gran'mother Doom'll have something to say about that.
Flora Then Elfine must simply avoid Aunt Ada. Which oughtn't be difficult — she never leaves her room.

Seth laughs

Cousin Seth?

Neck enters

Neck Don't let him go! Just don't let that boy —
Flora One moment, please! (*To Seth*) Cousin Seth ...

Reuben enters, running

Reuben Miss Flora! Miss Flora!
Flora Cousin Reuben? How did you —
Reuben 'Tes Grandmother!
Flora What about her?
Reuben She do be 'olding The Counting!
Flora The Counting?! Tonight?
Elfine Oh!
Reuben Aye! And she be screaming for 'er mommets!

Flora (*to Seth*) Did you know about this?

Seth laughs

Then you're a crashing bounder!
Elfine Oh, Flora ...
Neck Seth, I gotta talk —
Flora Not now, Mr Neck! Elfine — buck up! We are, I'm afraid, for it.
(*To the audience*) And don't think *you're* getting away scot-free. We're
all in this together! Oh, and if any of you have an old-fashioned camera,
a tripod and a flash lamp do please produce them at once. The Counting,
I am sure, will provide ideal conditions for the "Let's-Pretend-To-Be-
A-Photograph"-type effect. Brace yourselves, now — Aunt Ada is
waiting!

Black-out

SCENE 2

The kitchen, set up for The Counting

*The sukebind has grown enormously, and is now in flower. The plant, in
blooming, has released its perfume and the sweet, sickly smell hangs
heavily in the air. (Perhaps incense can be burnt in the kitchen during the
interval.) Ada sits in an enormous high-backed chair. Urk lies on the floor,
face down and motionless. Rennet, in gum-boots, is huddled in a corner.
Amos kneels, mumbling prayers, with a magazine in his hands. Judith is
also present, as is the extended Starkadder family. These include: Mark
(Amos's half brother) and Phoebe Starkadder, and their three children—
Dandelion, Jane and Jacob. The children range from nine years old to
fourteen. Dandelion huddles behind Ada's chair, Jane is at Ada's feet, and
Jacob sits on Ada's knee. The following relatives cower about the kitchen,
all within Ada's sight: Michah Starkadder and his wife, Susan. (Michah
is Amos's cousin and Urk's father.) Luke (Amos's half brother). Sairy-
Lucy's Polly (Luke's daughter), her husband, Naphthalie, and their three
babies (dolls) in three appalling prams. Naphthalie's half sister, twice
removed, Sheba. Meg, an unmarried female whom nobody can remember
having been born of the Starkadders, but who quite certainly was. Meg's
twin, Peg. Various other Starkadders are also present*

The collected Starkadders play a vital role in this scene, contributing a variety of moans, murmurs, gasps and wails. Their principal reactions are included, but many more may be introduced; they should underscore the action almost constantly. Any periods of absolute silence are indicated

There is a deadly hush in the room; nobody says a word apart from Amos and Ada. Ada sings discordantly as she rocks Jacob to and fro. A single oil lamp hangs from one branch of the sukebind and illuminates Ada's face horribly. The fire gives a more than usually hellish glow, with lurid shadows

Ada (*looking up; to the audience*) Aye! Gather in around me — gather in! You're all mine! Mine! Ivery one o' you! And none o' you mun leave! (*She claws a hand into the air and draws it to her heart*)

A great groan from the Starkadders. The Lights fade further. Ada stands Jacob up

Jacob! Fetch me my copy of the *Milk Producers' Weekly Bulletin and Cowkeepers' Guide!*

The Starkadders mumble: "Milk Producers' Bulletin", "Cowkeepers' Guide", etc. Judith moves forward to Amos and snatches the bulletin from his hands

Amos 'Tes gone! Lord! 'Tes a sign! A sign!
Ada Amos!

Amos clasps his hands and returns to his quivering

Judith 'Ere ...

Judith gives the magazine to Jacob, who moves fearfully toward Ada and, trembling, holds it out toward her. Ada takes the magazine. She rolls it into a tight tube, and the Starkadders twist and groan as she does this. She gives a final twist to the magazine; the Starkadders convulse. Jacob bursts into tears

Ada Silence!

She clubs Jacob with the magazine and he falls to the floor, unconscious. There is a gasp from the Starkadders. Ada looks around. Silence. Phoebe now dashes forward and tries to pick up her son. Ada points at her with the rolled-up magazine

Phoebe ...

Phoebe lays her son, the sacrificial lamb, down again. She withdraws, weeping. Ada points at her with the magazine

Phoebe!

Phoebe stands up straight

Starkadders Phoebe.

Ada now scans the room, picking out the Starkadders with the magazine and calling their names. They each stand up and move forward when called

Ada Mark!
Starkadders Mark.
Ada Luke!
Starkadders Luke.
Ada Judith!
Starkadders Judith.
Ada Amos!
Starkadders Amos.
Ada Susan!
Starkadders Susan.
Ada Michah!
Starkadders Michah.
Ada Sairy-Lucy's Polly!
Starkadders Sairy-Lucy's Polly.
Ada Sairy-Lucy's Polly's husband, Naphthalie!
Starkadders Sairy-Lucy's Polly's husband, Naphthalie.
Ada   Sairy-Lucy's Polly's husband Naphthalie's half sister twice removed, Sheba!

Starkadders Sairy-Lucy's Polly's husband Naphthalie's half sister twice
  removed, Sheba.
Ada Meg!
Starkadders Meg.
Ada Peg!
Starkadders Peg.
Ada Dandelion!

Silence

  Dandelion!

Dandelion, behind her at the chair, taps Ada on the shoulder

  Argh!

*Ada bludgeons Dandelion with the magazine, and she falls to the ground
with a moan. She lies unconscious on top of Jacob*

  Elfine!

Silence

  Elfine!

Silence

  Seth!

Silence

  Seth! Seth, Seth, Seth!

Silence. Ada throws herself back in the chair

  Argh! Woodshed, woodshed! Narsty! Narsty! Woodshed, woodshed!
  Narsty, narsty! Argh! (*She collapses, unconscious, in her chair*)

*A great commotion goes up from the Starkadders. Some of them edge
bravely forward, peering at Ada. Suddenly the door is thrown open and*

*a great gust of wind sweeps through the kitchen. The Starkadders moan
and retreat. Silence*

*Flora, Elfine, Seth, Reuben and Neck enter. Flora carries a tyre pump
and moves to Amos*

Flora *(whispering)* Cousin Amos — the pump for the tricycle.

Amos takes the pump gingerly

Well, well... *(To the audience)* The gang's all here!
Judith You must greet your Aunt Ada.
Ada I saw something narsty in the ——
Flora Yes, so I've heard.
Judith Mother, 'tes Flora Poste. Robert Poste's Child.
Ada 'Twas a burnin' noonday ... all them years ago. And me no bigger
than a titty-wren ...
Flora *(to the audience)* Not much of a conversationalist, is she?
Ada *(rising slowly from her chair and shuffling forward)* Seth? Where is
my Seth? Where is my darling boy?
Seth 'Ere, Gran'mother. 'Ere I am.
Ada Ah!
Seth And I will niver leave 'ee — niver ...

Judith moves toward Seth with a moan

Amos *(leaping at Judith)* Woman!

*Ada enfolds Seth in her arms. Seth contributes to the picture in a
statuesque manner. Neck moves to Flora*

Neck What a dude ...
Flora Quiet, Mr Neck!
Ada That's my boy ... my mommet ... my pippet ... Why, how grand he
is tonight! But what's this? What's all this? Where 'ave you been? What
'ave you been doing, boy? Tell your granny!
Flora He's been to Richard Hawk-Monitor's twenty-first birthday party.
And so have I, and so has Elfine, and so has my friend, Mr Neck. What's
more, Aunt Ada, Elfine and Richard are engaged to be married — and
will be, too. Just as soon as things can be arranged.

There is a terrible cry from Urk. He rises up from the floor

Neck What the ...?!

Urk steps crazedly forward. Rennet rushes to him with a pleading, strangulated moan. Urk throws Rennet aside, and she collapses with a shriek. Urk reaches out as if to throttle Flora

Ada I shall go mad! I shall go mad!

Urk suddenly collapses in tears

Urk My liddle water-vole!
Amos Lord!
Judith Seth! *(She rushes toward Seth)*

Seth throws her aside. There is a pained shriek from Judith and a chorus of despair from the Starkadders. Seth gives a wild cry and strikes a pose. Silence. Neck comes forward, making a screen shape with his hands and looking at Seth through it

Neck That's it, sweetheart! That's got it! Now — hold it!
Flora *(to the audience)* And Seth, soaked as he is in movie slang, holds it with perfection.
Neck Wow! Baby — would you like to be in the talkies?

There is a gasp from the Starkadders

Seth Me?
Neck Who else!
Flora Mr Neck is a film producer, Cousin Seth. He has a studio in Hollywood.
Seth Oh! Do 'ee know Lotta Funchal?
Neck Old Lotty? Sure I do! I got her under contract right now!
Seth Oh!
Ada I saw something narsty!
Neck You can meet her, if you want. Hey! She can be your first leading lady! Would you like that?
Seth Lotta Funchal! Oh! More 'an anythin' in the woarld!

Neck Well, ain't that dandy? He wants to be a movie star and I want to make him one!

Ada I saw something narsty!

Flora Cousin Seth, go to your room and pack at once. You're going on a long, long journey.

Amos Journey!

Judith No!

Neck Can it!

Ada I saw something narsty!

Neck You know, honey, someone oughta write you some new dialogue. Seth?

Seth looks from Judith to Ada and exits

Neck Attaboy!

Neck exits

Ada and Judith wail. Amos steps forward

Amos If a sinner can leave then so mun I!

Ada What?

Amos I mun go, I say! I mun go! For the Lord calls me to it and I mun obey!

There is a gasp from the assemblage

Ah, 'tes terrible a thing, but I mun do it! I 'ave been a-wrestlin' and a-prayin' and a-broodin' over it for months — and now I know the truth at last! I mun go abroad on one o' they nice ol' tricycles! A nice old tricycle — with a platform on the back! Aye, like the Apostles of old I 'ave 'eard my call, and I mun follow it!

Ada No!

Urk Elfine! Elfine!

Amos: He flung his arms wide, and stood with the firelight playing its scarlet fantasia upon his exalted face!	**Ada:** No, no! I cannot bear it! There have always been Starkadders at Cold Comfort Farm!	**Urk:** Me and the water-voles! We've failed!

We're beaten!

You must not go!

Lord! Lord!

Argh!

I hear the glad
voices of the
angels calling me!

We planned a nest for
her up by Nettle Flitch
Weir — me and the
water-voles — and
would have taken her
there when the egg-
plant was in bloom!

Out over the
ploughed fields!
Where the liddle
seedlin's are clappin'
their hands in prayer!

And now she has
given herself to him—
Richard Hawk-

You must not!

Monitor! When she
was but an hour old,

The tricycle do be
ready tonight!

None of you might
leave!

I did mark her feeding
bottle wi' water-vole's
blood. She was mine,

I've no time to lose!

I shall go mad! I
shall go mad! I saw
something narsty in
the woodshed!

see? Mine! And I've
lost her ... Oh, why
did I ever think she
was mine?

Ada Arghhh! There have always been Starkadders at Cold Comfort
Farm! But that means nothing to you! Nothing!

Amos Aye — *nothing*!

There is a gasp from the Starkadders

'Tes goodbye to you, Mother!

Ada Argh!

Amos 'Tes goodbye to you *all*!

Silence

Flora (*to the audience*) Ada's eyes, like slots of pain in her grey face, turn
fiercely upon Amos; they blaze with hate!

Reuben comes forward with Amos's hat, coat, and warming pan

Amos (*snatching the hat, coat, and pan*) Aye — with the help o' the angels
   and the Lord's word ——
Flora (*to the audience*) No mention of me, of course.
Amos — I have broken your chains — forever!
Ada A-m-o-s!
Flora (*to the audience*) A screech from her heart roots that buries itself
   in his plexus. But he does not turn. He goes to the door, throws it
   wide ——

There is a great gust of wind through the kitchen as Amos opens the door.
The Starkadders shriek. Mark and Michah rush to restrain Amos, but he
throws them off. Susan rushes to her husband

  Amos exits

Ada Amos ...

  Mark, Michah and Susan charge out after him

Reuben shuts the door

Flora (*to the audience*) — and is gone.
Ada Argh! (*She swoons*)

Judith and Rennet rush to catch her

Judith Mother!
Ada Alone! Alone ...!
Urk Aye! But I'll not be alone!

There is a gasp from the Starkadders

  I will not!
Flora (*to the audience*) He is laughing noiselessly, insanely!

Urk laughs — noiselessly, insanely

Urk Come 'ere Rennet! Aye! I 'ave lost Elfine but I shall not be alone!
I 'ave lost my mommet — but I shall take 'ee instead!

*Seth enters, wearing a coat and carrying a suitcase. Neck enters behind
him*

Ada Seth!
Neck Well, well ... how's the girl?
Ada I saw something narsty!
Neck Did *it* see *you*? Seth?
Urk Aye, dirt as you are, I'll take 'ee, and we'll sink in the mud together!
Ada You must not take her, Urk! I forbid it!
Rennet Oh? And what's it to do wi' you?

There is a gasp from the Starkadders

Aye, gasp if you must, but I 'ave found my voice — and I mean to use
it!
Judith Seth! Seth! You must not go! 'Twould break my 'eart! Besides,
there's the spring onions to bring in.
Neck Gee, ma'am, I know it's raw, I know it's tough — but that's life, girl!
Rennet Right then, Urk; I'll 'ave 'ee, my angel — and to 'ell wi' Mark
Dolour!

There is a great gasp from the crowd. Urk gives a wild laugh

Judith No, no!
Neck Look, baby — why not come along with us? I'll get you a job. As
my secretary! How about that?
Judith Why must you take him? Why? Why?
Neck OK ...

Neck pulls Seth in front of Judith

Now you see this hunk, honey?

Judith sobs

You know what this hunk has got?

Judith moans

He's got passion!

Judith wails

And do you know what passion is?
Judith I know nothing! I am a dead woman! A broken chaff! A used
   gourd!

Neck grabs Judith and kisses her passionately

Neck That's passion!

Judith is stunned. She stares at Neck, transfixed

And that's what sells pictures. And your boy here has got passion by the
sackful — and the looks. *That's* why I need him! *That's* why I can't give
him up! See?

Judith, unable to speak, simply stares at Neck

OK, OK — he'll send you five grand out of his first picture. How's that?

Pause

Judith exits

Urk Come then, my beauty — my handful o' dirt!

*He throws Rennet over his shoulder. There is a spontaneous round of
applause from the crowd*

Rennet And who's coming with us?
Ada No-one, no-one!

*But as Urk makes toward the door with Rennet he is followed by a train
of squealing Starkadders; this includes everybody in the room apart*

from Ada, Reuben, Elfine, Seth, Neck and Flora (Phoebe snatches up Jacob and Dandelion on her way)

Argh! Come back! Come back! You must not leave me!

Flora (*to the audience*) Ada Doom stands bolt upright, her eyes closed tight against the world. She is rigid. Her lips move, softly. I listen, and can just make out what she is saying. It is none too festive.

Seth (*moving to Flora*) I jus' wan' t' say — thank 'ee. Thank 'ee — and goodbye.

Neck Come on, baby. I tell you sweetheart, you're going places — and you ain't never coming back!

Seth and Neck exit, leaving the door open

It appears that only Flora and Ada are left in the room; in actual fact Reuben is standing in a shadowy corner and Elfine is asleep in a chair, but we can see neither of them very clearly. Flora crosses to the door and closes it. Silence and stillness. Judith now enters from upstairs wearing her coat and carrying a suitcase and her photograph album

Judith Where did he go?

Flora Who?

Judith My man! My man! My *beautiful* man!

Flora Oh, really, Cousin Judith — we've been through all this. (*She takes the album*) Cousin Seth has gone to be a film star.

Judith Nay — not Seth! (*She takes the album back*) I am not talking about Seth! Seth is my son — nothing but a capsy boy-child. Nay — I am talking of the American gentleman!

Flora Mr Neck?

Judith He has asked me to go away with him. I am his passion!

Flora Well, I'm not sure that's quite what he ——

Judith He has asked me! He is very kind. There is a dark force in him. It beats like a black gong! I wonder you cannot 'ear it.

Flora We can't all strike it lucky.

Ada groans a little

Judith Goodbye Mother! (*She throws the album on to the fire*)

A red glow leaps across the room. Ada trembles. Judith steals toward the door. As her hand touches the latch, Ada lets out a great screech

Ada J-u-d-i-t-h!

Judith stops and looks back at Ada. The fire and the red glow subside. Pause

Judith exits, closing the door quietly behind her

Ada gibbers

Flora (*to the audience*) So Judith has gone as well — and I didn't have to lift a finger! (*She glances at Ada*) Oh, I say! What a picture! Yet still no sign of the old-fashioned camera, the tripod and the flashlamp. How very puzzling. Mind you, it is not yet "The End" — and "The End" is where a "Let's-Pretend-To-Be-A-Photograph"-type effect truly belongs — isn't it?
Reuben (*coming forward*) Do 'ee think Father'll return?
Flora Not a chance, my lamb. The farm is all yours now. All of it. Not that this kitchen looks too pretty at the moment. If only I had some snowdrops. Snowdrops would dispel this dismal atmosphere in a trice.
Reuben Snowdrops?
Flora Yes. Quite the most beautiful of flowers, don't you think? Still — Elfine ... Elfine ... wake up my lovely — it's time for bed.

Elfine takes Flora's hand and lifts herself drowsily

Elfine, Flora and Reuben exit

Ada is now alone. She stands, rigid, in the middle of the kitchen. The Lights fade, extremely slowly, until Ada is lit only by a tight pool of light

Ada Amos ... Urk ... Seth ... Judith ... All — gone. Gone ... And who was it that sent them away? Who was it that made 'em go? That brat! That wennet! Robert — Poste's — Child!

Lights out on Ada

The cowshed

We hear Adam crooning as a tight pool of light comes up around him. There is a light-filtering-through-cowshed effect. Adam carries a bucket

Adam (*singing*) Rooksies and Barnsies
               Do fly 'ome like charmsies,
               And the Tigget nor Teazle
               Mun chaff nor the winde.
  My birdling ... my mommet ... did I cowdle thee in my arms ... for this?

Rennet enters wearing gum-boots

Rennet Mornin' Adam.
Adam Why do 'ee break into my sorrow and my cowshed?
Rennet I be looking for a bucket for some rather narsty jam that I 'ave suddenly learned 'ow to make.
Adam 'Ave 'ee 'eard? Elfine is to be married — to Mus' Richard!
Rennet Aye. And you mun give 'em your blessing, I say.
Adam What?
Rennet Well, look at me an' Urk. Rooksies an' barnsies do fly 'ome like charmsies — so there's not a lot you can do about it, is there?

  Rennet takes the bucket and exits

Adam thinks for a moment, then notices that the bucket is no longer in his hands. He falls over with a moan. Black-out

The kitchen

The Lights come up to an early-dawn-on-Midsummer's-Day effect

Flora enters

Flora (*to the audience*) The dawn of Midsummer's Day. The dawn of

Elfine's wedding. I, myself, have had a very troubled night. Indeed, I
have not slept a wink for the last two weeks. Ever since the Counting,
a fortnight ago, I have done nothing but scan, and scan again, the pages
of *The Higher Common Sense* in an effort to find some answer to the
problem of Ada Doom. My aunt, you must understand, post Counting,
went flop into a conniption, retreated to her room, and has been neither
seen nor heard of since. Were the reception to be held at the farm, of
course, Aunt Ada would be simply bound to come downstairs — if only
to devastate the whole affair with her deranged shenanigans. As it is the
party will quite certainly take place at the Hall — well beyond the clutch
of her meddlesome hand.

Elfine enters

Elfine Oh, Flora! The wedding reception's to be held at the farm! Mrs
Hawk-Monitor says it will be so much more convenient than the Hall.
What's the matter?
Flora The whole place must be disinfected, of course.
Elfine Oh, I'll help. Don't worry.
Flora No, Elfine. The responsibility of the bride, on such an occasion, is
to go for a long and meditative walk. Preferably with a labrador.
Elfine I haven't got a labrador.

Flora takes a comb from her work-box and shows it to Elfine

Flora Then take from my work-box the large but delicate tortoise-shell
comb. Allow both it and your gentle fingers to work upon the appearance of your hair — just as the bright sunlight kisses the trees and works
upon the appearance of the land. I, meanwhile, must heave-ho with the
carbolic.
Elfine But you can't do it all on your own!
Flora I do not intend to do any of it, Elfine. And certainly not on my own.
(*She opens the door*)

The Chorus enters

Chorus A warm breeze moves across the meadows and a heavy dew rests
upon the downs.
Flora There we are, you see. Perfect conditions for a meditative walk.
Run along now, Elfine.

Elfine Oh, the comb! (*She picks the comb up from Flora's work-box, and also produces the copy of* Mansfield Park) What's this?

Flora *Mansfield Park*. A novel by Miss Austen.

Elfine One of the pages is turned down.

Flora I was reading the book before I came here.

Elfine Might I borrow it when you've finished?

Flora I shall not return to the book, Elfine, until my labours at the farm are complete. And there are one or two labours still to be grappled with.

Elfine Gran'mother Doom?

Flora Run along now, Elfine.

Elfine exits

(*Opening* Mansfield Park; *reading*) "It was over, however, at last; and the evening set in with more composure to Fanny ..." (*To the audience*) Dear Fanny Price. What a strange little heroine she is. I wonder what *she* would have made of Aunt Ada?

A member of the Chorus attracts Flora's attention

Oh, I'm so sorry. (*To the audience*) In the kitchen all is activity and expurgation.

There is now a great deal of activity on the part of the Chorus. During the following dialogue they execute a complete and utter transformation of the kitchen. The table is moved against a wall. The chairs are placed in front of it in a row facing outwards so that they act as both seating and as a large "step" by which one might climb on to the table. The old clock is replaced with a new clock of a clean, art deco design with a very long, elegant pendulum. Initially, the pendulum remains immobile. The Lighting reflects the changes, moving from the misty haze of morning to the full blaze of a golden afternoon

For the rest of the scene the characters speak exclusively to the audience unless it is noted otherwise

Chorus The old clock, at last, is taken away for scrap — and a new one put in its place. Pink and white rose-peonies are delivered by the basketful. Adam Lambsbreath makes his own contribution: wreaths of daisies with which to garland the horns of the cows. It is not until he actually tries to affix these decorations, however, that he realizes that none of the cows have any horns left. Linen is unpacked, silver polished, and a variety of crockery clettered — with Adam's little mop.

Flora I, myself, am indifferent to these activities. I have returned, in desperation, to *The Higher Common Sense.*

The Lights come up on Ada (above)

Ada Flames of hate flicker across my citadel ...
Flora (*reading*) "Never arrive at a house at a quarter-past three ..."
Ada 'Ow can I be 'appy, now that I am old?
Flora (*reading*) " ... it is a dreadful hour ..."
Ada 'Ow can I be 'appy, now that I am alone?
Flora (*reading*) " ...too late for luncheon and too early for tea."
Ada 'Ow can I be 'appy now that Robert Poste's Child ... Robert Poste's Child!!
Chorus The sky grows blue and sunny.
Ada The insolent summer beats at my windows ...
Flora (*reading*) "Can we be sure that an elephant's real name ..."
Ada ... but the curtins ...
Flora (*reading*) " ... is Elephant?"
Ada ... as 'ave hung at these windies these last siventy years ...
Flora (*reading*) "Only mankind presumes to name God's creatures ..."
Ada ... keep out the light and leave cold the old and crumbling tower o' my body.
Flora (*reading*) "God himself is silent upon the matter."
Chorus The kitchen continues to buzz with energy.
Ada I press myself into the armour o' my corsets!
Chorus Outside, in the cowshed, Sairy-Lucy's Polly whisks sillabubs into a frenzy.
Ada Now — my elastic-sided boots!
Chorus Michah delivers pails of ice — with which to cool the champagne.
Ada I saw something narsty!
Chorus Glasses are polished ...
Ada Niver told Mamma.
Chorus ... napkins folded ...
Ada Something I saw ...

Chorus ... and tiles, once dead, are scrubbed back into life.

Ada A prickly beard, a smell o' flannel, a stumblin', urgent voice.

Chorus The chairs are rearranged.

Ada My boots smell narsty. Elastic! Narsty! Where be the lavinder water?

Chorus The table is covered in a clean white cloth and moved back against a wall to create more room.

Ada Now my peddicoats ...

Chorus A hundred jam-jars, jugs and vases are dusted down and filled with water.

Ada Now my gloves ...

Chorus Floors swept and windows cleaned.

Ada Now my blouse ...

Chorus Luke is outside fixing an awning across the front of the farm house.

Ada Now my first skirt ...

Chorus Below this awning is placed a trestle-table ...

Ada Now my leggins ...

Chorus ... from which refreshments are to be served.

Ada Now my second skirt ...

Chorus These refreshments are of two kinds — as befits the two sorts of guests expected. For the Starkadders, and such of the thorny peasantry as will attend, there are ice puddings, caviar sandwiches, crab patties and trifle. For the County ...

Ada Now my knickers!

Chorus ... there is cider and bread.

Flora (*reading*) "Beware the straw in the gaoler's hand — it tempteth, yet is false." Oh, really — this is useless! Quite, quite useless!

The Lights fade on Ada

Insane Agricultural Matriarchs, it seems, are emphatically beyond the reach of all Common Sense — Higher or not!

Lighting increases on the kitchen, as the transformation is now complete

Chorus A hush now falls upon the cool, flower-garlanded, sweet-smelling farm. The sun climbs royally to its zenith. The shadows grow longer.

Flora (*to the Chorus*) Yes, but you've done nothing at all about the sukebind! (*She opens the door*) Goodbye.

The Chorus exits

Flora turns back into the room. She looks about and is pleased

(*Noticing the clock*) Oh, really! (*She goes to the clock and sets the pendulum moving*) There!

SCENE 5

The kitchen

The clock ticks sweetly. Flora notices Mansfield Park, *picks it up and reads*

Flora "It was over, however, at last ..."

Ada enters

Flora does not see Ada, but senses her presence and turns

Oh.
Ada Robert Poste's Child!

The clock explodes

I — am — mad!
Flora Really? (*To the audience*) But I have noted already her firm chin, clear eyes and tight little mouth. If she's mad — I'm one of the Marx Brothers. (*To Ada*) I'm so glad to see you up and about again, Aunt Ada. Have you decided to come to the wedding?
Ada Weddin'! (*She inhales with a shudder of rage*)
Flora Perhaps not.
Ada I saw something narsty! Aye! And smelled it too! Smell! Sniff! Dubbin on leather! Beeswax on strap! Niver spoke of it though — not even to Mamma ... but I remember ... That is what 'as made me ... diff'rent. That is what did blight mun own marriage; 'orrifyin' nightmare as it was for me!
Flora Did you ever ask your husband how he felt about it?

Ada Even now, though I be past my ripeness, I cannot pass a woodshed
— nor even a boat-'ouse neither, funny enough — without a terrible
sickenin' piston a-plungin' in my sinews! That is what did make me
bring mun children into this world with venom! And with loathin'! But
they 'ave all gone now! All of 'em! Save Elfine! You shall not take
Elfine! She is mun wash-pot, mun sloose-bottle — and I 'ave cast my
shoe out over 'er!

Flora I feel I must point out, Aunt Ada, that this kind of outburst has no
effect upon me whatsoever. My temperament, like my life, is a tidy one.
You, of course, are not fond of tidy lives. Oh, no. Storms are what you
like. Plenty of spite. Doors being slammed and partings forever ——

Ada And eyes dartin' like bruised thoughts! Tortured sperm-trout in their
pools o' pain!

Flora I will not rise to these antagonisms. I never do. But be warned, Aunt
Ada; I like nothing more than pitting my cool will against an excitable
opposition. And I do not like my enemies to win.

Ada Nor me, neither!

Flora Then one of us will just have to get used to it — won't she, Aunt
Ada?

Ada You think you're cliver, doan't 'ee! A-stealin' away mun family!

Flora None of your family has been "stolen away" ——

Ada But there be somethin' you've forgotten ——

Flora — by me or anbody else.

Ada — for all your cliverness!

Flora What do you mean — something I've forgotten?

Ada laughs with a wild, deranged, triumphant cackle

Why are you laughing in that ridiculous manner?

Ada Amos!

Flora Cousin Amos was far from amusing.

Ada And Judith!

Flora In fact he was thoroughly miserable.

Ada Both stolen away! Gone! No longer 'ere! (*Another cackle*) Aye! And
by the 'and o' Robert Poste's Child 'erself!

Flora Cousin Amos and Cousin Judith left this farm quite of their own
volition. As did all the others. As, indeed, with Elfine; if I have anything
to do with it.

Ada You shall not take Elfine!

Flora On the contrary, Aunt Ada; *you* cannot keep her.

Ada Oh, can't I? Can't I, then — Robert Poste's Child? (*She bursts into a crazed conniption of ecstatic laughter, gesticulating with wild glee. She concludes her outburst with a shriek of anger, and looks at Flora for a response*)

Pause. Flora bursts into a crazed conniption of ecstatic laughter, gesticulating with wild glee. She concludes her outburst with a shriek of anger. Ada stares at Flora

Flora Yes, you see — I can do it, too. But I choose not to. In very much the same way as you choose to be mad. Yes — choose. You have chosen, Aunt Ada, just about the most convenient form of madness possible. Oh, yes! It allows you absolute control with not a whiff of responsibility! Oh, you can shriek and gesticulate as derangedly as you please! Gibber in dialect 'til the cows come home — with or without their horns; but from me, Aunt Ada, you cannot hide the fact that you are a shrewd old bird, as calculating as an abacus, with a determined mind as sharp and as penetrating as a needle! But I have rescued Elfine from you — and there is nothing you can do about it. She will marry Richard — she *will* — and she will bear him a fine family of pleasant, ordinary, acceptable children. She will not bear them with venom and with loathing; nor with any sort of piston plunging in her sinews. She will bear them with love! These children may, of course, burn a little with poetry in their secret souls — but that is only to be expected, and not entirely without merit. But not for one instant will your artificial lunacy cloud their sunny lives! I have prised open your visor, old woman — and there is nothing there! This is my Victory! Lay down your malice and accept defeat! For my hands are on the handles of the sword, and I shall not turn back! Besides — if I did Charles would make a particular sort of face ...

Ada Charles?

Flora My victory is Elfine and my victory is in sight! My victory is a victory of dignified application! My victory, Aunt Ada, is the victory of Civilized Thought over your own grubbing philosophy of farmyard and bin! My victory is a splendid deer stepping haughtily over a ploughed field!

Pause

Ada Your victory is nothin'! (*She laughs, quietly, knowingly*) You still doan't see it, do 'ee? Amos! Judith!

Flora Both gone; yes, I know.

Ada Aye! And where does that leave Elfine — with both 'er parents nowhere about the place? Who is it now as becomes 'er legal guardian? Legal! Who is it now that she mun plead with for consent to marry? And who is it, do 'ee think, as'll niver give it?! (*She breaks into more deranged laughter*) And 'twas *you*, Robert Poste's Child, as did send 'em away! Hah! You 'ave plunged your sword into your own 'eart! (*She laughs. Pause*) Well?

Pause. Flora fetches her flying suit

Flora Goodbye, Aunt Ada.

Ada Eh?

Flora Your strategy is impeccable and your power absolute. I don't stand a chance. Have I your permission to leave?

Ada stares at Flora

Thank you. (*She makes to leave*)

Ada Well, that weren't much fun ...

Flora Fun? Is *that* what you want?

Ada I want to rest. I want the sun. I want an 'Arvey Wallbanger ... 'Tes terrible exhaustin' bein' a total recluse.

Flora Then why go on with it?

Ada What else am I to do?

Flora Oh dear, sweet, adorable Aunt Ada. If you won't come to the wedding, won't you at least attend the party afterwards? Come now, my dove; why not put on something pretty, rearrange your face into a more symmetrical pattern, and grace the reception as the endearing old grandmother you surely are? Elfine, I know, would so like it if you did; and you, I am sure, would find it a very happy occasion.

Ada Argh!

Flora (*to the audience*) Oops ...

Ada 'Appy!

Flora (*to the audience*) Clearly not her favourite word.

Ada 'Appy!

Flora (*to the audience*) And I was doing so oozingly well — don't you think?

Ada 'Ow can I be 'appy, now that I am alone? 'Ow can I be 'appy, now that I am old?

Flora "Is Youth the sole recipient of Joy? If so — why smiles the Sphinx?"

Ada Smiles? Smiles? My face doan't smile! Least, not symmetrically ... It shall die in its ugliness — alone!

Flora Neither you nor your face are going to die at all — at least not for a very long time.

Ada But it shall! *I* shall! I shall die upstairs, old an' alone — with narsty things pressing upon me!

Flora Oh, very well then.

Ada Eh?

Flora Die.

Ada What?

Flora Go on — die. And liberate Elfine!

Ada Nay! I shall not!

Flora Fiddlesticks.

Ada I shall live! Forever!

Flora (*to the audience*) It never rains but it pours.

Ada And I shall niver give mun consent to Elfine! Niver! Niver! Niver!

Ada exits with a great screech of laughter

Flora sighs and looks about the room despairingly. She sees the copy of Mansfield Park *and picks it up*

Flora Oh, Charles ... (*She reads*) "And the evening set in with more composure to Fanny ..." Mmm ... lucky Fanny. Just a moment! With more composure to Fanny! Fanny! Fanny! Oh, why didn't I think of it before! Now — where's my copy of *Vogue*? Oh, Charles! Charles! What a miracle you are! (*She rummages through her work-box and finds the copy of* Vogue) Here we are! Now then ... Fanny ... Ah! "Beauty and Joy for Those No Longer Young." Oh, and there's a photograph of her! Excellent! (*She reads*) "Miss Fanny Ward — shining example of the thoroughly reformed recluse!" Splendid! And such a radiant and infectious smile! "Miss Ward recommends a combination of sloth, alcohol, and a European climate." Of course! Now then ... the brochure ... (*She produces the Mirimar Hotel brochure from her work-box*) A-ha! (*To the audience*) If this doesn't work — then I'm a Dutchman! (*She calls*) Aunt Ada? Aunt Ada!

She exits with the brochure, Vogue, *and her flying suit*

Ada (*off*) Argh! I saw something narsty! Narsty, narsty, narsty!
Flora (*off*) Yes. But now you're going to see something very, very nice.
Ada (*off*) Nay! (*Pause*) Ooo ...!

A great shaft of Light now bursts into the kitchen, accompanied by a euphoric chord from an organ. The Light is absolutely brilliant, coloured like the stained glass windows of a church. The Light strikes the sukebind and the plant, with a last desperate moan, withers, crumbles and dies. Under cover of the music the sukebind is cleared away

SCENE 6

Howling Church

The music stops. Silence. We hear a wedding march while the Lights dim so that the stained glass window effect is prominent

Richard enters wearing a morning-suit and a top hat. He is accompanied by Sneller, similarly dressed. They stand at the table. Mrs Hawk-Monitor, beautifully dressed and crying, enters and stands a little below Richard

Other guests arrive. The County are dressed extremely smartly. The Starkadders have done their best. They stand in two groups — the Starkadders on one side, the County on the other to form a centre aisle

The music pauses, then starts up again

Elfine enters wearing the most beautiful wedding dress and carries a snowdrop bouquet. She is accompanied by Reuben and they process to the table. The bridesmaids (Jane and Dandelion) enter carrying Elfine's train. She arrives at the table and the music stops

Flora enters wearing an elegant outfit. She carries an old-fashioned camera, a tripod and a flash-lamp. She acknowledges this to the audience and sets up the camera

Flora (*to the audience*) The little church is full of people, but it is the presence of the Starkadders about which I am most delighted. They are all here, you see, *all* of them, by *my* agency. And they are *enjoying* themselves. Having a nice, ordinary, human time — in a nice, ordinary, human manner. They are not mollocking somebody, or beating somebody, or having religious mania. Neither are they being doomed to silence by a gloomy, earthy pride, nor are they loving the soil with the fierce desire of a lecher. No — they are simply enjoying an ordinary human event, like millions of other ordinary people all over the ordinary world. (*To the assembly*) Say "Cheese"!
All Ch-e-e-se!

Flora lets off the flash. The actors freeze, pretending to be a photograph. It would be nice if this effect can really be bumped up somehow

Flora (*to the audience*) Perfect!

Church bells ring out. The people on the table climb down into the kitchen. The crowd mills about, chatting. Flora gets rid of the camera equipment

SCENE 7

The kitchen

Sneller and Adam dispense the drinks

Rennet (*approaching Flora*) Should I take some weddin' cake up to the ol' monster? Keep 'er quiet, like?
Flora Thank you, Rennet, but if you could just make up a Harvey Wallbanger ...
Rennet Eh?
Flora The orange is on the draining board, and the vodka under the sink.
Rennet Well ... if you say so, Cousin Flora.
Flora I do, No-Longer-Daft Rennet. Oh, and Rennet?
Rennet Yes.
Flora Our nice new clock has suffered a little in transit. Please have it repaired and set in motion at once.
Rennet 'Twill be done — you can rely on it.
Flora Oh, I do hope I can ...

Mrs Hawk-Monitor (*embracing Dandelion*) Why, Dandelion! Dandelion! And did you enjoy being Auntie Elfine's bridesmaid? (*To Elfine*) Elfine, my precious! How beautiful you look! And how lucky Richard is! It's quite delightful — the whole thing! (*She kisses Elfine*)

Adam approaches with a small parcel of newspaper

Adam A weddin' present for 'ee, maidy. A gift for my daffodowndilly ...
Elfine Oh, Adam ... marsh-tigget's eggs; four of them!
Adam Aye. Put 'em in they bosom and 'twill make 'ee bear four children.
Flora Yes, Adam — but not before she's had something to eat ...

Flora sweeps Elfine away

Elfine Oh, Flora — I can hardly believe it! Mrs Hawk-Monitor is positively transformed! She has been calling me "her precious".
Reuben (*approaching Flora*) Cousin Flora?
Flora Reuben?
Reuben Might I talk to 'ee a moment?
Flora If it's about the swede harvest ——
Reuben On your own, if I may.
Flora Why, yes ... yes, of course.

Elfine moves off. Reuben puts down a chair

Flora Whatever is it, Cousin Reuben? You look quite pale.
Ada (*off*) So here you all are!

The crowd looks off with a roar of amazement

Ada enters dressed in a flying suit. She is wreathed in peonies and looks fantastically glamorous

Welcome to Cold Comfort Farm! (*She moves forward*)

The crowd parts, Red Sea-like. Rennet presents the Harvey Wallbanger to Ada, curtsies and retreats. Ada swoops on Mrs Hawk-Monitor. The crowd gathers about Ada, astounded and entranced

Mrs Hawk-Monitor, I presume?

Mrs Hawk-Monitor Dear me ... how splendid ... so unexpected and ...
How do you do, Aunt Ada ... or should I say, Mrs Doom?
Ada Nay, you mun say what 'ee likes! Aye, and do what 'ee likes, an' all.
For that's how I mean to be from now on! Free! Free as a bird!

A questioning ripple runs through the crowd

That's right! I fly to the South of France at any moment!

There is an astonished reaction from the crowd

Fanny Ward 'as nothin' on me!

The crowd gives a great cheer. Sneller whispers to Ada

Ladies and Gentlemen! Buffet ... is served!
Flora (*to the audience*) And the happy crowd files out to feed beneath the
awning.

Most of the guests exit

Ada (*to Flora*) However can I thank 'ee, mun pippet?
Flora Your happiness, Aunt Ada, is thanks enough. I only hope you like
it.
Ada Livin' up in them mountains at the 'Otel Miramar? Ooo, 'twill suit
me down to the ground! A-loungin' by that pool all day and sippin' on
mun cocktails! And 'tis all thanks to 'ee, mun dear. A-makin' me see
what a lovely time can be had in this world by a sensible old lady of
good fortune, a firm will and an almost symmetrical face! Ooo! 'Twill
be such fun!
Flora And fun, Aunt Ada, is all you've ever really wanted, isn't it?
Ada Hush, mun lovely! That be our little secret. Now then, my dove, what
pretty thing shall I send you from France?
Flora Oh, there's really no need —
Ada Piff! Now — what shall it be?
Flora Very well. A work-box, please. Mine is rather wearing out.
Ada A work-box? So be it.
Flora But Aunt Ada, there is something else you can do for me, too —
if you will.
Ada What's that, mun trinket?

Flora Well ... Could you tell me, please ... what *was* the wrong that Judith's man did to my father? And what are my "rights"? Please forgive my curiosity, but I feel I have to ask.

Ada glances about, then whispers to Flora. Pause

Flora Oh. And did the goat die?

Elfine approaches with Adam. Adam carries the wooden leg

Elfine Grandmother, Adam wants to come and live at Hautcouture Hall.
Ada By all means, mun dear!

Adam squeals with delight

Ooo, but Adam — who shall care for Graceless if you go? I shouldn't like to have to sell 'er.
Adam Nay! Niver say that, Mrs Starkadder, ma'am! I'll take her wi' me. Aye, and Feckless, Pointless and Aimless, too.
Ada But ...
Adam There's room for us all at 'Owchicker 'All!
Ada Very well, Adam; you mun take the cows if you wish!
Adam Oh, Bless 'ee, Mrs Starkadder ma'am! Bless 'ee. Graceless?

Adam exits

Elfine Oh, Grandmother! What a lovely old lady you are. (*She kisses Ada and moves off*)
Flora And did the goat die? Aunt Ada!
Ada I'm sorry, mun chirip?
Flora The goat! Did it die? And what about my "rights"? You haven't said a word about my "rights"!

There is the sound of an aeroplane landing off stage

Ada Oh, that'll be my aeroplane! So kind of your Mr Neck to arrange all this for me! Goodbye mun spangle — and thank 'ee! Thank 'ee! Thank 'ee over a thousand times!
Flora But ...

Ada exits, followed by the remaining crowd

(*To the audience*) So my questions are unanswered. And are destined to remain so now.

Off stage there is a cheer from the crowd and the sound of the plane moving overhead. NB This is distinctly different from the sound of Charles' craft

(*To the audience*) I am delighted, of course, that Aunt Ada should be flying into a fun-packed future in the South of France, but I can't help feeling a bit disappointed about my "rights" — and about the goat.

Elfine enters carrying her bouquet

Elfine I shall be gone in a moment, Flora. Richard is waiting in the car.
Flora Dearest Elfine, I do hope you shall be very, *very* happy.

Pause. They embrace, both a little tearful

Run along, my dear. Your life is about to begin.

Elfine smiles and makes to leave

Elfine (*turning back*) Oh, Flora? Catch! (*She throws her bouquet to Flora and smiles*)

Elfine exits

Flora (*to the audience*) Snowdrops?

Off stage there is the sound of a car starting up. The crowd cheers and the car moves off

Reuben enters with two pieces of wedding cake

Reuben Cousin Flora?
Flora Oh ...
Reuben Some weddin' cake for 'ee.
Flora Oh. Thank you.

Reuben looks at Flora

Is there something the matter? Oh yes, of course — plates. (*She finds two plates and a vase and puts them on the table. She puts the bouquet in the vase*)

Reuben looks at Flora

What is it? Oh, I think we can use our fingers — just this once.

Reuben Who was you telephonin' this afternoon?

Flora Pardon?

Reuben You was telephonin' somebody. From the post office — near the church.

Flora Oh. Oh, yes.

Reuben Who was you telephonin'?

Flora Charles.

Reuben Charles?

Flora Yes, he's ... he's a friend of mine. Aren't these snowdrops beautiful? Where could they have come from, do you think? At this time of year?

Reuben I grow'd 'em. In a special bulb-box.

Flora Oh, Reuben ... But where on earth did you get the money for a special bulb-box?

Reuben I did falsify th' chicken books. I bin doing it for years.

Flora My dear, I think you're masterly! Quite masterly!

Reuben Do 'ee?

Flora Oh, wonderfully so! With tricks like that you'll make the farm *too* prosperous. Oh, this cake is delicious!

Reuben Cousin Flora?

Flora Mmm?

Reuben I doan't suppose 'ee would marry me, would 'ee?

Pause

Flora (*taking Reuben's hand*) Oh, Reuben, that is nice of you. But I'm afraid it would never do, you know. I am not at all the kind of person to make a good wife for a farmer.

Reuben I like your priddy ways.

Flora And I like yours. But really ... I think someone like ... like Dandelion, would be much nicer for you. And much more useful, too.
Reuben Dandelion bain't fifteen yet.
Flora All the better. In three years' time the farm will be so very well, and you will have a really lovely home to offer her.

Pause

Reuben (*withdrawing his hand*) Aye—m'be I would be best wi' Dandelion ... And if she won't 'ave me, there's always — Mark Dolour.

Reuben exits

Flora (*to the audience*) And the last of the Starkadders is gone.

The Lights change subtly. Flora fetches her suitcase and work-box. She moves about the kitchen, looking at things and touching them gently

(*To the audience*) It is with a feeling of satisfaction, and even something strangely like affection, that I now glance about the place. Cold Comfort Farm, you see, no longer looks like a beast about to spring. Not, of course, that it ever has done to me, for I am not in the habit of thinking things look exactly like other things which are as different from them as it is possible to be. (*Pause*) But it did once look dirty and miserable and depressing — and now it doesn't. (*She sees the clock, which has not been set in motion*) Oh, Rennet ... (*She goes to the clock and sets the pendulum swinging*)

The clock ticks, regularly and slowly

(*Making a final adjustment to the bouquet of snowdrops*) And I did all this — with my little hatchet.

Soft beams of opalescent sunlight filter through the windows. From outside, a long, long way off, there is the faint chime of cow bells

Adam has hung bells round the necks of his cattle, and has at last attached the wooden leg to Graceless's stump. He is taking her up to Hautcouture Hall. The old man's face is lifted to the sinking sun and its strong rays turn him to gold.

The chiming bells fade gently away

The kitchen is quiet and empty. All is cool. All is blessedly peaceful. The air chills — slowly. There is not a breath of wind. The shadows grow longer. The countryside is falling asleep. A cold, fresh smell comes up from the grass and falls from the trees. The flowers close, but give their fragrance still. The birds begin their sleep song. It is the loveliest hour of the English year: seven o'clock on Midsummer Night.

The clock chimes out, gently, the hour of seven. The Lights fade on the kitchen until it is bathed only in the pale wash of early evening. There is the faint sound of an aeroplane, which grows gradually louder. The aeroplane moves over the farmhouse, lands, and taxis across a field outside. The headlamps throw light into the kitchen. The light fades. The engine stops. Flora stands. Pause

Charles enters, exactly as at the beginning

In the sky above the kitchen a full and golden moon appears. A host of tiny stars begin to twinkle. Pause

Charles Have you done the "Let's-Pretend-To-Be-A-Photograph"-type effect?

Flora Some time ago, now.

Charles Then your campaign is at an end?

Flora Yes.

Charles Flora ... This is forever, isn't it? You and me, I mean?

Flora Oh Charles, you do smell nice. Is it the stuff you put on your hair? Yes, my darling — of course it's forever.

They go to kiss

Flora (*stopping*) You know, Charles — you have the most heavenly teeth ...

They kiss

... and I am glad I was born.

Charles I think we should go home now, Flora — don't you?

*Flora smiles and nods. Charles takes her suitcase and moves to the door.
Flora takes her work-box, looks about the kitchen and follows Charles.
Charles opens the door, and a broad shaft of golden moonlight spills in.
Flora gasps, faintly. She moves to the doorway and, bathed in moonlight,
looks up into the night sky*

Flora Tomorrow will be a beautiful day!

*She clasps her work-box tightly and exits. Charles also exits, leaving the
door open*

The kitchen is bathed in gold. All is tidy, pleasant and comfortable. Silence

*There is the sound of an aeroplane being started, followed by a low drone
as it taxis along the field. Suddenly there is a great surge as the aircraft
lifts off, moves directly overhead and fades to a murmur. In the sky, against
the stars, we see the tiny bi-plane. It moves gently past the moon and
disappears*

*Silence, apart from the ticking of the clock. The Lights fade slowly,
extremely slowly, on the kitchen, lingering for a moment on the clock and
the vase of snowdrops. The Lights fade gently on the vase. A pool of light
remains on the clock. The stars continue to twinkle overhead. The clock
explodes*

Black-out

*The company comes on to take a call. We hear folk music and the
company performs a frightening country dance (possibly involving a
few unwilling members of the audience). The company then takes a final
call*

CURTAIN

*NB It would be nice if, as the audience leaves the theatre, they find a huge,
illuminated hoarding outside advertising Seth's first film, "Small Town
Sheik". This should be made up of an enormous picture of Seth and his
leading lady, Miss Lotta Funchal*

FURNITURE AND PROPERTY LIST

ACT I
SCENE 1

On stage: Wooden table
Six chairs
Fireplace
Spit. *On it:* water-voles
Sink
Large clock
Sukebind plant

Off stage: Work-box. *In it:* Letter, copy of *Mansfield Park*, copy of *The Higher Common Sense* (Flora)
Suitcase (Flora)
Flying helmet (Flora)
Brochure for the Hotel Miramar (Neck)
Copy of *Vogue* (Charles)

SCENE 2

On stage: As before

Off stage: Candle (Judith)
Work-box as before, plus a postcard and pencil (Flora)

SCENE 3

Off stage: Bucket (Adam)
Wooden leg (Adam)

SCENE 4

Set: Loaf of bread and knife on table
Kettle

Off stage: Bunch of twigs (Elfine)
Dead mammals (Urk)

Scranlet (**Reuben**)
Wooden leg (**Reuben**)
Pair of net curtains (**Flora**)
Work-box as before, plus spring, screwdrivers, and pliers (**Flora**)
Tray. *On it:* Four sausages, a crocket of marmalade, a bowl of porridge, five fried tomatoes, a kipper, a teapot, nine boiled eggs (**Adam**)
Warming-pan (**Amos**)
Pot of porridge (**Rennet**)
Bowls (**Rennet**)
Spoons (**Rennet**)
Empty tray (**Adam**)
Parcel. *In it:* Gum-boots (**Reuben**)
Photograph album (**Elfine**)
Yoke with two pails of milk (**Rennet**)
Tea (**Rennet**)
Teacups (**Rennet**)
Teaspoons (**Rennet**)

Personal: Pack of cards with pictures of women (**Seth**)

Scene 5

Strike: Loaf of bread and knife from table, kettle

Off stage: Battery operated candle (practical) (**Flora**)
                Work-box as before (**Flora**)

Scene 6

Set: Warming-pan
                Black coat and black hat in cupboard

Off stage: Sukebind-tidying equipment (**Adam**)
                Tricycle wheel (**Reuben**)
                Parcel. *In it:* Dish mop with a red ribbon tied to the handle (**Reuben**)
                Gold-trimmed envelope (**Urk**)

Scene 7

On stage: Piano/pulpit affair

Off stage: Warming-pan (**Amos**)
                Tricycle with a platform on the back (**Flora and Elfine**)
                Buckled and broken warming-pan (**Amos**)

ACT II
Scene 1

Off stage: Drinks (Sneller)
              Elfine's and Flora's coats (Seth)

Scene 2
Set: Three appalling prams with three dolls (Sairy-Lucy's Polly)

Strike: Warming-pan
              Black hat and black coat from cupboard

Off: Magazine (Amos)
              Tyre pump (Flora)
              Amos's hat, coat and warming-pan (Reuben)
              Suitcase (Seth)
              Suitcase (Judith)
              Photograph album (Judith)

Scene 3

Off stage: Bucket (Adam)

Scene 4

Strike: Three appalling prams with three dolls

Off stage: Work-box as before, plus tortoise-shell comb (Flora)
              New art deco clock with pendulum (Chorus)
              Mops, brooms, dusters, brushes, etc. (Chorus)

Scene 5

Off stage: Flying suit (Flora)
              Work-box as before (Flora)

Scene 6

Off stage: Old-fashioned camera (Flora)
              Tripod (Flora)
              Flash lamp (practical) (Flora)

Personal: **Elfine:** snowdrop bouquet

SCENE 7

Set: Two plates, vase

Off stage: Drinks (Sneller and Adam)
               Small parcel of newspaper. *In it:* four marsh-tigget's eggs (Adam)
               Harvey Wallbanger (Rennet)
               Wooden leg (Adam)
               Two pieces of wedding cake (Reuben)
               Work-box as before (Flora)
               Suitcase (Flora)

Personal: Wreath of peonies (Ada)

LIGHTING PLOT

Interior and exterior settings
Practical fittings required: "flickering" battery operated candle

ACT I, Scene 1
To open: The reddish and unnatural glow of a dying fire

Cue 1	After a moment *Flash of lightning*	(Page 1)
Cue 2	**Ada:** " ... in the woodshed!" *Lightning*	(Page 1)
Cue 3	Bi-plane engine sound *Plane headlamps illuminate the kitchen*	(Page 1)
Cue 4	**Charles:** " ... a romance?" *Lightning*	(Page 2)
Cue 5	**Charles:** " ... beautiful golden hair." *Lightning*	(Page 3)
Cue 6	**Charles:** " ... Howling, Sussex." *Lightning*	(Page 3)
Cue 7	**Judith:** "Judith Starkadder ..." *Lightning*	(Page 4)
Cue 8	**Flora:** "... imperceptibly towards eve." *Bleakly-waning-moon effect*	(Page 7)

ACT I, Scene 2
To open: As before

Cue 9	Door is blown open *Lurid red glow from the fire; lightning*	(Page 9)

Cue 10	Seth sinks his teeth into a water-vole	(Page 10)
	Lightning; Black-out	

ACT I, Scene 3
To open: Bring up sallow-dawn effect

No cues

ACT I, Scene 4
To open: Bring up stifled-morning effect

Cue 11	Flora: " — down toward Mock Uncle Hill —"	(Page 22)
	Lights change abruptly	
Cue 12	The clock chimes four o'clock	(Page 28)
	Lights change to bloodstained-sunset effect	

ACT I, Scene 5
To open: The lights begin to fade slowly

Cue 13	Flora switches on the candle	(Page 31)
	Spot on Flora to cover candle	
Cue 14	The clock chimes midnight	(Page 31)
	Fade lights further	
Cue 15	Clock chimes the twelfth time	(Page 31)
	A shaft of moonlight catches the clock and falls across the sukebind	
Cue 16	The clock ticks	(Page 31)
	Shadowy lights on Ada	
Cue 17	Doors and windows bang	(Page 32)
	The candle gutters a little	
Cue 18	The clock explodes	(Page 35)
	Black-out; cut the candle and covering spot	
Cue 19	The Starkadders and Ada exit	(Page 35)
	Spot on Flora	
Cue 20	Flora: "All right? Good."	(Page 35)
	Bring up lights a little	

ACT I, SCENE 6

| | | |
Cue 21   The clock explodes   (Page 36)
Bring up lights to fecund-spring-day effect

ACT I, SCENE 7
To open: General interior lighting

Cue 22   Urk shrieks and collapses   (Page 45)
Black-out

ACT II, SCENE 1
To open: General effect of evening light; chinese lanterns (practical)

Cue 23   Flora walks about a little   (Page 54)
Chinese lanterns go off gradually; bring up pale-moonlight effect

Cue 24   Flora looks up into the night sky   (Page 55)
Gentle twinkle of shimmering stars

Cue 25   Flora: " — Aunt Ada is waiting!"   (Page 56)
Black-out

ACT II, SCENE 2
To open: Hellish glow from the fire with lurid shadows; oil lamp (practical)

Cue 26   A great groan from the **Starkadders**   (Page 57)
Fade lights further

Cue 27   Judith throws the photograph album on the fire (Page 67)
A red glow leaps across the room and then subsides

Cue 28   Ada stands alone in the middle of the kitchen (Page 68)
Lights fade slowly until Ada is lit only by a tight pool of light

Cue 29   Ada: "Robert — Poste's — Child!"   (Page 68)
Black-out on Ada

ACT II, SCENE 3
To open: A tight pool of light comes up around **Adam**; bring up light-filtering-through-cowshed effect

Cue 30	Adam falls over with a moan *Black-out*	(Page 69)

ACT II, SCENE 4
To open: Bring up early-dawn-on-Midsummer's-Day effect

Cue 31	The Chorus transforms the kitchen *Slowly bring up golden-afternoon effect*	(Page 71)

Cue 32	Flora: " ... *The Higher Common Sense*." *Bring up lights on* Ada	(Page 72)

Cue 33	Flora: "Quite, quite useless!" *Fade lights on* Ada	(Page 73)

Cue 34	Flora: " — Higher or not!" *Increase lights on kitchen*	(Page 73)

ACT II, SCENE 5
To open: As before

Cue 35	Ada: "Ooo ...!" *A great shaft of coloured light strikes the sukebind*	(Page 79)

ACT II, SCENE 6
To open: Fade lights to accentuate stained-glass window effect

No cues

ACT II, SCENE 7
To open: General interior lighting

Cue 36	Flora: "And the last of the Starkadders is gone." *The lights change subtly*	(Page 86)

Cue 37	Flora: " — with my little hatchet." *Soft beams of opalescent sunlight filter through the windows*	(Page 86)

Cue 38	The clock chimes out seven o'clock *Fade lights to the pale wash of early evening*	(Page 87)

Cue 39	The aeroplane lands *Headlamps illuminate the kitchen*	(Page 87)

EFFECTS PLOT

ACT I

Cue 1	To open *Distant rumbles of thunder; feeble wind; doors and* *windows rattle and bang*	(Page 1)
Cue 2	Lightning *Ferocious crack of thunder*	(Page 1)
Cue 3	Lightning *Thunder: after a moment, a distant bi-plane engine*	(Page 1)
Cue 4	Headlamps illuminate the kitchen *Cut bi-plane engine*	(Page 1)
Cue 5	Lightning *Thunder*	(Page 2)
Cue 6	Lightning *Thunder*	(Page 3)
Cue 7	Lightning *Thunder*	(Page 3)
Cue 8	Lightning *Thunder*	(Page 4)
Cue 9	**Flora:** " — bless you, my love." *Bi-plane takes off; engine fades*	(Page 7)
Cue 10	**Flora:** "Thank you." *Kitchen clock chimes*	(Page 7)
Cue 11	**Flora:** " ... at least the clock's working." *The clock explodes*	(Page 8)
Cue 12	**Flora** takes the candle and exits *Door is blown open by a gust of wind*	(Page 9)

Cue 13	Lightning	(Page 9)
	Thunder	
Cue 14	**Rennet** screeches	(Page 10)
	Splash off stage	
Cue 15	Lightning	(Page 10)
	Thunder	
Cue 16	**Black-out**	(Page 10)
	Fade storm effects	
Cue 17	**Reuben** enters	(Page 12)
	Pained lowing from Graceless off stage	
Cue 18	**Flora:** "Why on earth —?"	(Page 13)
	Blast of wind through the door as **Amos** *enters*	
Cue 19	**Rennet** screeches	(Page 15)
	Splash off stage	
Cue 20	**Flora:** "Oh, I see ..."	(Page 16)
	Pained lowing from Graceless off stage	
Cue 21	**Adam** enters with the empty tray	(Page 17)
	Pained lowing from Graceless off stage	
Cue 22	**Rennet** screeches	(Page 25)
	Splash off stage	
Cue 23	**Reuben** exits	(Page 25)
	Kettle whistles	
Cue 24	**Rennet** screeches	(Page 27)
	Splash off stage	
Cue 25	**Flora:** "... the dying day."	(Page 28)
	Clock chimes four o'clock dolefully	
Cue 26	**Ada** wails	(Page 30)
	The clock explodes	

| *Cue* 27 | **Flora** switches on the candle | (Page 31) |
| | *Clock chimes midnight* | |

| *Cue* 28 | Clock chimes the last time | (Page 31) |
| | *Eerie wind; the clock ticks slowly* | |

| *Cue* 29 | **Ada** exhales | (Page 32) |
| | *Wind moves through the kitchen; doors and windows bang* | |

| *Cue* 30 | The sukebind begins to move | (Page 32) |
| | *Loud creaking; ropes snap; padlock and chains shatter* | |

| *Cue* 31 | **Ada** takes a deep breath | (Page 34) |
| | *Wind moves through the kitchen* | |

| *Cue* 32 | **Starkadders** and **Ada**: "... in the woodshed!" | (Page 35) |
| | *The clock explodes* | |

| *Cue* 33 | **Flora** and **Chorus** exit | (Page 36) |
| | *The clock explodes* | |

| *Cue* 34 | The lights come up | (Page 36) |
| | *Twittering of birds; bleating of sheep* | |

| *Cue* 35 | **Elfine**: "Oh, Flora, Flora ...!" | (Page 40) |
| | *The clock explodes* | |

ACT II

| *Cue* 36 | To open | (Page 47) |
| | *Gentle waltz music* | |

| *Cue* 37 | **Sneller**: " ... Miss Block." | (Page 47) |
| | *Cut waltz music* | |

| *Cue* 38 | **Mrs Hawk-Monitor** nearly passes out | (Page 49) |
| | *Dance music begins* | |

| *Cue* 39 | **Flora**: "I ask for nothing more." | (Page 50) |
| | *Cut dance music* | |

| *Cue* 40 | **Mrs Hawk-Monitor**: "So ageing and putting off ..." | (Page 54) |
| | *Faint dance music* | |

Cue 41   Chinese lanterns go off   (Page 54)
              Music fades

Cue 41   To open Act II, Scene 2   (Page 56)
              Sweet, sickly smell of the sukebind (incense)

Cue 42   Door is thrown open   (Page 59)
              Wind sweeps through the kitchen

Cue 43   Amos opens the door   (Page 64)
              Wind sweeps through the kitchen

Cue 44   Flora sets the pendulum swinging   (Page 74)
              The clock ticks sweetly

Cue 45   Ada: "Robert Poste's Child!"   (Page 74)
              The clock explodes

Cue 46   Ada: "Ooo ...!"   (Page 79)
              Euphoric organ chord; music to mask the scene change

Cue 47   To begin Scene 6   (Page 79)
              Cut masking music; after a moment, a wedding march

Cue 48   The guests separate to form a centre aisle   (Page 79)
              Pause music; after a moment, start up again

Cue 49   Elfine arrives at the table   (Page 79)
              Cut music

Cue 50   All: "Ch-e-e-se!"   (Page 80)
              Flash

Cue 51   Flora: "Perfect!"   (Page 80)
              Church bells

Cue 52   Flora: " ... about my 'rights'!"   (Page 83)
              An aeroplane lands off stage

Cue 53   Flora: "And are destined to remain so now."   (Page 84)
              The aeroplane moves overhead and fades

Cue 54   Flora: "Snowdrops?"   (Page 84)
              A car starts up and moves off

Cue 55	**Flora** sets the pendulum swinging *The clocks ticks regularly and slowly*	(Page 86)
Cue 56	**Flora:** " — with my little hatchet." *Faint chime of cow bells*	(Page 86)
Cue 57	**Flora:** " ... turn him to gold." *Chiming bells fade*	(Page 86)
Cue 58	**Flora:** " ... seven o'clock on Midsummer Night." *The clock chimes seven o'clock*	(Page 87)
Cue 59	The lights fade *The sound of an aeroplane moving overhead and landing.* *The engine stops*	(Page 87)

Cue 60	A moment after Charles exits
	 The sound of an aeroplane starting up, moving forward
	   and lifting off. The plane moves past the moon
	   and disappears
		(Page 88)

Cue 61	The lights fade on the vase *The clock explodes*	(Page 88)
Cue 62	The company comes out to take a call *Folk music*	(Page 88)

Printed in May 2022
by Rotomail Italia S.p.A., Vignate (MI) - Italy